MAKERS
of the
MUSLIM
WORLD

Nasser

MAKERS
of the
MUSLIM
WORLD

Nasser

Hero of the Arab Nation

JOEL GORDON

ONEWORLD
OXFORD

Oneworld Publications
185 Banbury Road
Oxford OX2 7AR
England
www.oneworld-publications.com

ISBN 10: 1-85168-411-5
ISBN 13: 978-1-85168-411-3

Typeset by Sparks, Oxford, UK
Cover and text design by Design Deluxe

For Alex

CONTENTS

ACKNOWLEDGMENTS

This book is the product of many years of writing – and think-ing – about Nasser, his generation and his era. Many people, including some of Nasser's closest collaborators and some of his most bitter opponents (sometimes one and the same) have helped form my sense and sensibility of Nasser and Nasserism. Their input has been acknowledged in my earlier writings and they are, of course, all absolved of direct complicity in what is always a subjective analysis of history – in this case a history that is still very politically charged.

Special thanks for helping me script and score Nasser over recent years go to Ahmad Abdalla and Mahfuz Abd al-Rahman, Martin Stokes, Walter Armbrust, Israel Gershoni, and Elliott Colla. Farid al-Salim provided a second set of ears and some native proficiency for the anthems quoted in the text. I really want to thank Patricia Crone for enticing me to undertake this project, and all the people at Oneworld who have helped along the way.

NOTE ON TRANSLITERATION

Transliteration of Arabic names and terms follows the system adopted by the *International Journal of Middle East Studies*; however initial `ayans have been omitted to make the text more reader-friendly to non-specialists. Wherever possible, common popular spellings have been adopted for individuals – like Nasser – who are well-known. In keeping with colloquial Egyptian pronunciation, the more formal Arabic *j* has been replaced with the Egyptian *g*. Thus, *Gamal,* as he was to his people, rather than *Jamal.*

INTRODUCTION:
BELOVED OF MILLIONS

Gamal, beloved of millions – Gamal!
We're marching in your footsteps – marching – Gamal.
We're rising toward the light – we're advancing toward the
good.
We're with you, beloved of millions!
We're the millions – we're the millions!
[*Ya Gamal ya habib al-malayin*/Gamal, Beloved of Millions,
1958]

A midsummer night in July 1958, the Officers Club in
Cairo, under the stars. Egypt's luminaries – politicians
and military commanders, musical and film stars, literati and
selected foreign dignitaries – have gathered for a gala concert.
It is the sixth anniversary of the 23 July 1952 military coup,
the "July Revolution" that toppled Egypt's monarchy and overthrew the corrupt, failed liberal order.

A lot has happened in the interval. Four years later almost to
the day, on 26 July 1956, the anniversary of the forced exile of
the ill-fated King Farouk, the revolutionary regime proclaimed
full sovereignty over the Suez Canal and nationalized the multi-
national company that oversaw passage through the waterway
and collected tolls. That audacious act, coming as a total surprise to all but a select few, fomented an international crisis
and a Middle East war and made Egypt's young leader, Gamal
Abd al-Nasser, a national hero and regional sensation. This
year, Revolution Day is a time to reflect on another dramatic
step. Five months earlier, in February 1958, Nasser accepted
Syria's call for unity and established the United Arab Republic,
inaugurating a new pan-Arab phase in Egypt's revolution.

Ya Gamal ya habib al-malayin will premier at a gala outdoor performance to mark the Revolution's anniversary. Sung by Egypt's brightest new star, the "Brown Nightingale," twenty-seven-year-old Abd al-Halim Hafiz. The anthem speaks of a moment of national and regional triumph. The musical ensemble begins and the chorus, male and female, takes up the refrain. Reed-like in his black tuxedo, Halim steps to the microphone to take up the main theme:

> We're awakening the East in its entirety — its valleys and
>   mountains.
> Founded on its people, its heroes.
> With the hero of the Arab nation — we're the millions.
> In light, blessing and freedom — we're the millions.
> Gamal, beloved of millions.

This anthem is relatively short, about seven minutes. In succeeding years, particularly during the socialist sixties, songs and performances will become increasingly elaborate as Egypt's best lyricists, composers and artistic directors compete for prime time in national festivals.

This song stands out in the huge canon of Nasser-era anthems for the direct, unabashed — and unashamed — evocation of the leader. Other anthems pay direct homage, for example *Ya Ahalan bil-ma`arik* (Welcome, the Battle) from 1965, in which Abd al-Halim sings: "Our beloved Abd al-Nasser stands amongst us and addresses us." More often, the anthems play off the attributes associated with his names: beauty (*gamal*) and victory/the victorious (*nasr/nasir*). These songs reflect the spirit of the era that has come to be known as the "age of Nasser." They were reinforced by official and popular icons — statues, posters, commemorative coins, key chains, fountain pens and comic strips — icons that all but disappeared from the streets in the years following Nasser's death but which still lie scattered in private homes, shops and offices. No contemporary Arab ruler — or any who followed — could lay claim either to his panegyric titles or the resilient reservoir of goodwill harbored by "the millions" throughout the Arab world.

Gamal Abd al-Nasser, son of a minor postal official, ruled Egypt for eighteen years, three as unofficial head of a military junta, the rest as president. His biography meshes first with Egypt's early twentieth century liberation struggle, then with the battle to build an economically independent sovereign nation guided by principles of social justice. Nasser fought in one regional conflict (the 1948 Palestine War) and presided over three others: the 1956 Suez War, in which he spun military defeat (despite heroic resistance) into diplomatic victory, the five-year Yemen Civil War, which he referred to as his Vietnam, and the 1967 June War that threatened to undo his entire project. In his last years, before a heart attack felled him at fifty-two, he appeared prepared to reconsider fundamental precepts of his revolution, the socio-political order that had become known as *Nasserism*. That would be left to his successor, comrade-in-arms and fellow conspirator, Anwar al-Sadat. That Sadat undid so much of the Nasserist agenda in Nasser's name still incites heated debates about what might have been, if Nasser had lived into the 1970s and beyond.

Thirty-six years after Nasser's death, the images evoked in fiery nationalist anthems and socialist choreographies – proud peasants reclaiming arid desert lands, heavy machinery damming the powerful waters of the Nile to install electricity-producing turbines, soldiers marching smartly alongside military hardware bearing the tricolor republican Egyptian flag – seem tired, overwrought clichés. The very act of writing panegyrics to a leader or revolutionary state may appear gloriously anachronistic, even absurd. Nasser and his age long ago receded into a past that predates the vast majority of Egypt's – and the Arab world's – increasingly youthful population. Many of the social and economic transformations envisioned and haltingly undertaken by Nasser and his comrades have been undone. Egypt's post-colonial experience, since Nasser's last years, has been marked increasingly by disappointment and disillusion, defeat and despair. The optimism engendered by the destruction of an old order and birth of a new era has too often been replaced by the pessimism of those who decry the persistence of a political system rooted in the power of an authoritarian strongman. In the half century since the abolition of the monarchy Egypt has been effectively ruled by just three men: Nasser (1952–70) and Sadat (1970–81), who led the military uprising that evolved into a revolution, and Hosni Mubarak (1981–present), who rose to political prominence from the officer corps and has ruled continuously under martial emergency provisions. In such a historical context, how can Egyptians look back to the old anthems and iconography with anything but cynicism?

Nasser and his era remain pivotal to Egyptian, Arab, Middle Eastern and post-colonial world history. As his closest confidant, the journalist Muhammad Hasanayn Haykal (known to many English-language readers as Mohammed Heikal) has often noted, Nasser was a man both of great achievements and great failings. This view has perhaps become a cliché, a rationalization of errors; yet it reminds us how momentous were the dreams and aspirations of newly independent Afro-Asian nations, how charismatic many of those who led national liberation struggles and how difficult the obstacles they encountered in a bipolar world in the new nuclear age.

In a global context, Nasser and Nasser's Egypt are best studied in the context of Nehru's India, Sukarno's Indonesia, Nkrumah's Ghana, Tito's Yugoslavia, (as well as Ho Chi Minh's Vietnam and Castro's Cuba): fellow leaders with whom the Egyptian ruler rubbed shoulders and with whom he forcefully advocated international recognition of the concerns and agendas of new states. In the Arab world, Nasser had many rivals but few peers. Those rivals, wrote a contemporary observer, "always lived in his shadows" for, among other reasons, he "always possessed a certain moral advantage over them." [1]

---

[1] Malcolm H. Kerr, *The Arab Cold War: Gamal Abd al-Nasir and his rivals, 1958–70* (London: Oxford University Press, 1971), p. 154.

The dominance of Egypt over Middle East politics, both blessing and curse, was unmatched in the fifties and sixties. Nasser became the iconic Arab ruler, even if in some neighboring countries those icons had to be kept hidden from local authorities. For many outside the Middle East, he remains the epitome of the desire of Arab authoritarian rulers (such as Syria's Hafiz al-Assad, Libya's Mu`ammar al-Qadhafi or Iraq's Saddam Husayn) to exert personal influence throughout the region. All have been accused of, or credited with, trying to become the "new Nasser" of the Arab world.

Such assessments, both of Nasser and his anointed imitators, are often expressed in terms of stark ambition on behalf of self and nation, with nation and ruler inextricably linked. Even the charisma of such figures, celebrated in retouched official portraits of power and overblown spectacles of legitimacy, is described in stark negative or satirical terms. There is a certain verity to such critical depictions, for Nasser as well as his imitators, yet to focus solely on the facade is to miss the power of the charisma embodied in a figure like Nasser, particularly for his generation and time. Nasser's star fell steeply in his last years; it was then deliberately almost erased by his successor. Arguably the image was crafted by acolytes as well as honest adorers – and at times by former adorers, who had grown ambivalent about the revolutionary project and the persistent domination of the state by a ruler and his inner circle. None the less, the power of his personality and image remained remarkably resilient for two decades and the roots of that power are embedded in a real personality and biography.

Nasser was, to cite an old cliché, the "first Egyptian to rule Egypt since Cleopatra." Begging the issue of the last, tragic pharaoh's real cultural and geographic pedigree, Nasser was, if not truly a rural son of the soil, the progeny of unremarkable common people, caught up in the tumult of world wars, world depression and decolonization. His ability to master and shape that history, to capture public imagination and retain popular acclaim even in the face of setbacks and defeats speaks to the reality of much of his image. The majority, if never all, of Egypt's and the Arab world's millions referred to him as Gamal, Abu Khalid (following Arab custom, as the father of his eldest son) or *Rayyis* (boss), far more often than the more formal Nasser or Abd al-Nasser. He had enemies and detractors, those who feared him and those who loathed him, those who mistrusted him and those who judged him a disappointment, even a failure. Yet, if he failed to deliver on many of his promises, both spoken and those he embodied in his rise to power, for two decades he expressed the heart-felt aspirations of many during a vital, formative era of Middle Eastern history.

1958 represented a peak of this era, when Nasser truly was beloved by millions. In the previous five years he and his fellow revolutionaries had overthrown a corrupt political order, deposed a king who had become an international laughing stock and abolished the monarchy outright. Through careful guerilla warfare against British troops based in the Suez Canal Zone, as well as by cleverly endearing themselves to American diplomats, they had persuaded the occupier to sit at the bargaining table and negotiated evacuation. They had been courted by leaders of the non-aligned movement, frustrated Anglo-American efforts to foster a pro-Western defensive pact and, having been snubbed by the West when they sought to enhance their military capability, turned to the Soviet bloc to purchase arms. When Washington and London retaliated by withdrawing support for the High Dam at Aswan, the symbol of Egyptian revolutionary progress, Nasser played his trump card and nationalized the Suez Canal Company. When British, French and Israeli forces invaded Egypt, Nasser emerged unbowed, a *bona fide* Third World hero. By 1958, a pivotal year in the region's history, his stamp appeared everywhere: in the anti-monarchical revolution in Iraq, the civil war in Lebanon and the stirring of rebellion in Jordan.

In the midst of this he embarked on an ambitious gambit, tying Egypt's sovereignty to Syria in a United Arab Republic. Accustomed to the acclaim of the Egyptian street, in early 1958

Nasser found himself swallowed by equally enthusiastic throngs in Damascus. In photographs and newsreel footage, crowds line the route of his motorcade, almost as many packed on to

الرئيس جمال عبد الناصر

President Gamal Abdel Nasser

Le Président Gamal Abdel Nasser

The Rayyis. Official portrait of Nasser from the early 1960s. (Property of the author.)

the balconies as in the streets below. Nasser stands, waves and smiles. Heady days for a new nation, led by a former lieutenant colonel, the forty-year-old son of a postal clerk.

WE'RE THE PEOPLE: 1918–1956

We are your life and your smiles and you are our life,
We'll rejoice and you'll exult in our joy.
All that we extol, your heart will amplify our affection,
For we've chosen you and will march behind you,
The chief with the heart of gold, who has opened the gateways
   of freedom.
[*Ihna al-sha`b* (*We're the People*), 1956]

*I*hna al-sha`b, performed by Abd al-Halim Hafiz at Nass-er's inauguration on 24 June 1956 as Egypt's first elected president, is the first great anthem of the Nasser era. In the weeks and months after the Free Officers' take-over, almost all Egypt's poets and composers collaborated to produce patriotic songs extolling the virtues of what quickly became known as the "new era," well before the rebels had determined the extent of their political aspirations. For nearly four years, the political future remained uncertain. The young officers who had so boldly inserted themselves into the political arena, to inspire and, if need be, command reform, soon resolved that they alone could – and should – guarantee the revitalization of democracy. However, the old order, though dispirited and discredited, did not die easily. Other reformist agendas, some moderate, some more radical, contested the right to shape Egypt's future. Consequently, the Free Officers found them-selves compelled – some took to it more easily than others – to use martial force to insure that their evolving vision and their movement would persist. A crucial component of their re-invention of the state was the emergence of a bona fide leader to capture popular sympathy, a man who could and would stand above the collective and personify the nation.

Gamal Abd al-Nasser had been the driving force behind the Free Officers and he remained the most influential voice after 23 July 1952 in the new general command that ran the country. His imprint on the direction of what became the July Revolution is clear. Yet his emergence into the limelight, the headlines, was deliberate and his love affair with the masses slow to develop. Partly this was political sensibility; the country cried out for a reprieve from the politics of personality and was not ready to declare allegiance to an unknown, thirty-four-year-old colonel. Partly it was also disposition. Nasser had led the clandestine military movement from its inception but few in the organization even knew him as their leader. He was neither orator nor propagandist. Like his closest colleagues, he exuded great personal charm but his was a quiet passion. For three years after their take-over Nasser led from the shadows, working within a joint revolutionary command behind a figurehead leader. By 1955, however, his position both within the junta and in the public gaze was uncontested and his public persona, initially hard-edged, had begun to soften. By early 1956, he had become inextricable from Egyptian national, regional and international aspirations. His first uncontested election followed which, by formally legitimizing his authority, officially ended his long journey from the wings, on to center stage and into the hearts of the masses.

MODEST BEGINNINGS

Nasser was born on 15 January 1918, in Balos, a suburb of Alexandria, Egypt's second largest city. Like Anwar al-Sadat, his comrade-in-arms and eventual successor, Nasser would expand his rural roots into a key component of his native identity. Early biographies are replete with references to his *sa`idi* (Upper Egyptian) roots, a family tradition tracing his tribal lineage to Arabia and his indomitable character traits — inner fortitude, manliness, group solidarity, generosity and openness. Yet Nasser, like Sadat, was really a city boy. Many biographers note that he spent holidays in Bani Murr, his father's hometown, 250 miles from Cairo, which must have had a population of several thousand. To one biographer, Nasser admitted years later that he never visited his ancestral village until he was twenty, presumably when as a young cadet he took his first post at a nearby base.

If he was not truly a rural-born son of the soil, his paternal family origins were certainly rooted in the earth and his background far more modest than those of the social and political élite whom he would displace. Husayn Khalil, his paternal grandfather, who reputedly lived to the age of 107, was a peasant, although as the owner of five feddans (one feddan is roughly one acre) was hardly dirt poor. Two of Husayn's six sons, Abd al-Nasser and Khalil, left the village to be educated, took employment in the state bureaucracy and never looked back. Abd al-Nasser Husayn (1888–1968), Gamal's father, attended the *kuttab* (Qur'an school) in Bani Murr; later he was sent to Assiut, to attend a high school run by American Presbyterian missionaries. As a student in the provincial capital – Assiut at the time had a population of 30,000 – Nasser's father traded his *gallabiyya* (ankle-length gown) and *taqiyya* (skullcap) for a school uniform and *tarbush* (fez), the headgear of the modern middle class. As he worked his way up the civil service, Abd al-Nasser proudly maintained his new urban outfit; even after his son's revolution swept the *tarbush* from people's heads – not by decree but symbolic distancing from what many perceived to be a sartorial artifact of the old regime – the old man refused to abandon this mark of status.

After graduating from secondary school, Nasser's father entered the civil service. He found employment in Alexandria in the postal administration. In 1917 he married Fahima Hammad, the daughter of an Alexandria coal merchant, also with Upper Egyptian roots. Fahima, who was fifteen years his junior and financially secure, bore their first child, Gamal, within the year. When Nasser was three, his father was transferred to Assiut. It is difficult to imagine the family not visiting Bani Murr, although Gamal's recollections were hazy at best. Four years later, Abd al-Nasser was transferred to a village near Suez, in the Canal Zone. He surely sought more for his son than a rural education. Gamal, therefore, was sent to Cairo, to live with his paternal uncle, Khalil. With financial assistance from his father, seven-year-old Gamal entered the Nahhasin primary school in the heart of Cairo's bustling, medieval Khan al-Khalili district.

Separation from his family, which now included three younger brothers, probably deeply affected the young Nasser. Gamal corresponded with his mother, who he saw only during holidays. In the spring of 1926, her letters suddenly stopped. The family told Gamal his mother had taken ill and gone to stay with his grandmother in Alexandria. When he arrived home on a holiday trip, the eight-year-old learned that his mother had died. It was, as he recalled years later, "a cruel blow that was imprinted indelibly on my mind." [1] Less than two years later his father remarried; in 1929, upon a posting to Alexandria, he summoned the eleven-year-old Gamal to rejoin the family. Ethnographers insist that remarriage was not uncommon for men in Abd al-Nasser Husayn's position but Gamal never felt close to his stepmother and a barrier had risen between father and son that would never really be broken. Gamal started high school in Ras al-Tin, not far from one of the two royal seaside palaces. Four years later, in 1933, the family relocated again, when his father was appointed as postmaster in Cairo's working class Qurunfush district, between the medieval city and the modern district of Abbasiya, where many of Egypt's new army officers would soon take up residence. The family lived

[1] Robert Stephens, *Nasser: A political biography* (Middlesex: Penguin, 1971), p. 28.

in a traditional neighborhood, Khamis al-Ads, in a flat rented from a Jewish neighbor and next to a Kairite synagogue. Gamal attended the Nahda school but only just passed his exams. It was not due to lack of intelligence – "Gamal had plenty of that" – but rather to "an ingrained tendency to play truant, coupled with an early penchant for meddling in politics." [2] As for many of his contemporaries, formal schooling had become less important than the lessons of the street.

In high school, first in Alexandria, then in Cairo, Gamal began his political education. Nasser's generation came of age in the tumultuous thirties, the second decade of Egypt's faltering parliamentary experiment. The men who would ultimately overthrow the "liberal order" were born around the time of the 1919 revolution against British rule. Too young to remember it, they were raised with stories both of its glories and, increasingly, resentment towards its failings. Disillusion, staining the optimism of youth that drew them into the streets, would eventually turn them into soldiers committed to fostering their own revolution against those who had failed the nation.

FALSE HOPES

For many Egyptians, the 1919 revolution is still the crowning moment of Egyptian nationalist historiography. Britain occupied Egypt in 1882, ostensibly protecting European financial investments by ousting a reckless nationalist government, returning proper authority to the Ottoman-appointed *khedive* (viceroy) and reasserting foreign control over Egypt's economy. At first simply intending to restore order and leave, British politicians quickly determined their forces needed to stay for the long haul. Egypt remained an Ottoman realm, albeit dominated by the British agent and consul general, until the outbreak of World War One. When the Young Turk government in

---

[2] Joachim Joesten, *Nasser: The rise to power* (Odhams: London, 1960), p. 15.

Constantinople allied with the Central Powers, Britain unilaterally declared Egypt a protectorate, its *khedive* the sultan (and the British agent and consul general the high commissioner). After the war Egyptian nationalist leaders formed a *Wafd* (delegation) to petition the high commissioner for permission to present their demands at the Paris peace conference. When Sir Reginald Wingate ordered Wafdist leaders to be arrested and deported, the country erupted. Demonstrations and acts of sabotage against colonial outposts broke out in all sections of the population, as Egyptians transcended religious, class and gender boundaries to speak on behalf of a unified nation. In 1922, Sir Edmund Allenby, the man who had marched through Jerusalem to liberate Syria from Ottoman rule during the Great War, set in motion the processes for the establishment of a constitutional monarchy that would be independent, save for a series of British "reservations."

Born of popular uprising but assisted by colonial overlords, the new liberal order faced insurmountable obstacles. The 1923 constitution granted supreme power to the monarch – the sultan had become a king – who could dismiss parliament at his royal whim. Egypt's two kings, Fuad (reigned 1923–1936) and Farouk (reigned 1936–52) ultimately served British masters. Britain reserved the right to sovereign authority with regard to imperial defenses, communications, the Sudan and the rights of non-Muslim minorities and foreign interests. For the nationalists, the rallying cries became "total independence" from Britain and greater legislative and executive power from the monarchy. The *Wafd*, re-invented as a formal political party, could win an electoral majority but would only be allowed to form a government when it suited British or royal interests; this usually occurred when the *Wafd*, having been banned from or boycotted an election, mustered enough force in the streets to make its banishment from power untenable. A vicious cycle began in 1924, following the first democratically-held elections. In November 1924, after only eleven months of rule, Prime Minister Sa'd Zaghlul, the *Wafd* leader and hero of 1919, resigned in the face of British gunboat diplomacy following the assassination, by radical nationalists, of Sir Lee Stack, the British Commander-in-Chief of the Egyptian army and Governor-General of the Sudan. A series of minority governments followed, led by palace-appointed chief ministers, some sincere nationalists but all willing to collaborate with anti-liberal elements. Nasser would remember Zaghlul's death, when he was just nine years old; the outpouring of grief and the lingering resentment at his enforced expulsion from power.

By the early 1930s, Egypt's troubled parliamentary order faced a far graver crisis. The *Wafd* had formed only three governments – in 1924, 1928 and 1930 – and none had lasted more than a year. In 1930, the King appointed an autocratic loyalist, Ismail Sidqi, to head a minority coalition. Sidqi promptly abrogated the 1923 constitution and replaced it with a new charter that granted even greater authority to the crown. Demonstrations, of a kind not seen since 1919, erupted. *Wafd* partisans and minority parties battled in the streets. New forces, not directly affiliated with the parties but clearly linked to a growing sense of popular antipathy to establishment organizations, began to assert their authority, including the Islamist Muslim Brotherhood, founded in 1928, and the ultra-nationalist youth movement, Young Egypt, founded in 1933. Faced with mounting opposition, Sidqi's government collapsed in 1933. A new minority coalition restored the 1923 constitution but the King and his British backers acceded to popular demand and called for elections.

In 1936 the *Wafd* regained power and, with global war on the horizon, renegotiated the Anglo-Egyptian relationship. The treaty, approved by both governments, officially ended the occupation. Britain recognized Egyptian independence, agreed to an exchange of ambassadors and supported Egypt's membership of the League of Nations. Egypt agreed to allow Britain to maintain a 10,000-man military force in the Suez Canal Zone and bound itself to ally with Britain in case of war. Britain reserved the right to augment its military forces to safeguard Egypt from aggression and to reoccupy the country, should the need arise. The Montreux Convention of 1937, supported by Great Britain, approved a twelve-year phase-out of capitulations and mixed courts, extra-territorial privileges for foreign subjects that had been long decried by Egyptian nationalists. Two years later, the outbreak of World War Two would render Egyptian independence virtually meaningless but, for the moment at least, Egyptians could celebrate.

This was when Gamal Abd al-Nasser and his generation took their first political steps and threw their first projectiles at occupying forces and subservient Egyptian police. At the Ras al-Tin school in Alexandria, Gamal led the student movement. During his first demonstration he was struck in the face by a police baton and spent a night in jail. In November 1935, back in Cairo, he lost two friends to police gunfire and a bullet grazed his forehead. He was taken to the offices of an opposition newspaper to recover; the following day his name appeared in print as a wounded hero. At the time, he was drawn to the fiery rhetoric and martial spirit of Young Egypt. There is no indication that he joined the ranks of the green shirts, the *mujahidin* (fighters), but he may well have attended Young Egypt rallies, read the movement's publications and contributed a few coins to its "piaster plan" to help finance local industrial projects.

If formal classroom learning did not capture young Gamal's attention none the less, he had become an avid reader of literature and history. Nasser's generation of middle class, upwardly mobile students read both European and new Arabic literature. Gamal read biographies of Churchill, Bismark and Ataturk and wrote a junior-year essay on Voltaire; he also read Egyptian nationalist poets and essayists such as Ahmad Shawqi and Mustafa Kamil, as well as the prose fiction of Tawfiq al-Hakim, such as *Yawmiyat na'ib fil-aryaf* (Diary of a Rural Prosecutor), a biting satire of bureaucratic ineptitude and corner-cutting and *Awdat al-ruh* (Return of the Spirit), the tale of a young boy who discovers the deep roots of Egypt's civilization. Sometimes Egyptian nationalism trumped the Western masters: the bill for a high school production of *Julius Casear*, in which Nasser played the title role, championed the Roman dictator as the conqueror of Great Britain.

But what role to pursue? According to the 1936 treaty, the Egyptian military, formerly an arm of the British occupation, now served an independent state. The officer corps remained the province of the aristocracy, a "jigsaw puzzle of parade units, quasi-police forces and cavalry squadrons for polo-loving pasha's sons."[3] Family ties counted and tuition fees for the academy were prohibitive. However, plans to rapidly enlarge the armed forces and a desperate need for junior officers created new opportunities. Middle class sons of Nasser's generation answered that call. His applications to the military and police academies (he was decidedly less interested in the latter) were rejected, due to lack of connections and the record of his political activities. Gamal fell back on the university. He enrolled in the faculty of law but lasted only one term. Other future comrades fared equally badly; their minds were not set on academia. Persisting in his ambition to enter the military, Gamal managed (probably through his Uncle Khalil) to secure an interview with the Under-Secretary of State for War, who agreed to support his application. In March 1937, he began officer training, part of a cohort scheduled for an accelerated seventeen-month program.

NIGHTS AROUND THE CAMPFIRE

In the army Nasser found his calling. His grades were solid and his instructors recognized his leadership talents. Within six months he had been promoted and assigned as head of a study group. In July 1938, he passed his final exams and received his first posting, to Mankabad in Upper Egypt, not far from Assiut and Bani Murr. There, surrounded by fellow junior officers

[3] Jean Lacouture, *Nasser* (New York: Knopf, 1973), p. 41.

of like mind, the next phase of his life began. Anwar al-Sadat described Nasser as "a manly and straight-backed young officer ... reserved and serious in manner" and impatient with chit-chat and he denoted Mankabad as the birthplace of the secret society that would become the Free Officers. Published recollections of long days on maneuvers and long nights of political discussions around the campfire blur the edges of cliché: "We were young men full of hope. We were brothers-in-arm, united in friendship and in a common detestation of the existing order of things" but are surely rooted in reality.[4]

In early 1939, Nasser requested, and was granted, a transfer to the Sudan. There, he met up with Abd al-Hakim Amr, one of his study group charges at the academy and they became great friends. In May 1940, Nasser was promoted to lieutenant and in late 1941, assigned to El Alamein, where he was reunited with Sadat. In September 1942, he was promoted to captain; six months later he was appointed as instructor in the staff college at Abbasiya, on the outskirts of Cairo. In 1944, he married Tahiya Kazim, the younger sister of a friend of his Uncle Khalil; her father owned a small rug factory in Abbasiya. Four years his junior, Tahiya was educated and financially secure, thanks to an inheritance. In 1946 their first child, Hoda, was born; another daughter, Mona, followed a year later. Tahiya quickly sensed her husband's involvement in clandestine activities but even on the night of the Free Officers *coup* never realized his role as leader. Even when First Lady, she remained far from the spotlight, she rarely attended state functions and never exuded a sense of power or privilege.

Despite its formal independence, the Second World War accentuated Egypt's subservience to its British masters. Young junior officers like Nasser, who had graduated between 1937 and 1939, grew increasingly frustrated. The treaty bound Egypt to ally with and support Britain but palace politicians,

[4] Anwar al-Sadat, *Revolt on the Nile* (London: Alan Wingate, 1957), pp. 11–12.

keenly observing the course of the war, prevaricated and hedged their bets. Rumors of royal connections with Axis agents proliferated. As Rommel's Afrika Korps advanced through Egypt and many in Alexandria and Cairo loudly welcomed liberation, British officials lost patience. On 4 February 1942, British tanks surrounded Cairo's Abdin Palace and Britain's ambassador threatened to depose the young King if he failed to appoint a Wafdist government. At the nervous urging of his key aides, Farouk reluctantly signed. The incident was a watershed in Egyptian politics. The *Wafd*, although it never formally declared war against the Axis, sullied its image as the conscience of the nation. Farouk, momentarily an unlikely hero, soon spun out of control, gambling and womanizing in a way that long after marked his reputation and left some British officials wondering if they should not have carried out their threat to depose him. Hindsight proved that the British had acted precipitately, for within eight months Rommel's advance was first checked, then turned back at El Alamein.

The Egyptian army stood on the sidelines throughout the Second World War, as patriotic commanding officers sought avenues for political action. Some unit commanders in the western desert refused British orders to hand over their weapons in the face of Rommel's advance. Scattered groups began to organize, albeit a bit recklessly. In late 1941, Anwar al-Sadat and several colleagues unsuccessfully tried to assist a senior officer, the highly decorated Aziz al-Misri, to fly behind enemy lines and contact the German command. In Cairo, Sadat met German agents but was arrested and sentenced to prison. Other officers gathered secretly and circulated political leaflets. Their rhetoric reflected the growing concerns of the era: independence from foreign occupation and political and economic reforms that would produce a more stable and just society. Like Sadat and his friends, these officers quickly drew the authorities' attention. The junior officers who would later seize power pursued a more cautious path.

In 1943, or early 1944, Nasser, Abd al-Hakim Amr and several other future founders of the Free Officers, joined the secret military wing of the Muslim Brotherhood. The Brotherhood had become the largest, best-organized non-establishment opposition force in the country and, in the mid-1940s, began organizing clandestine cells within the police and military. To maximize membership it stressed patriotism over Islamism and did not insist on a full oath of fealty. Returned to Cairo from their various postings, Nasser and other associates met regularly under Brotherhood auspices. Some, but not all, became committed to the movement's broader agenda; others drifted away toward more secular, particularly left-wing, movements. For the present, in the final war years and the early post-war years of escalating political turmoil and social discontent, the Muslim Brotherhood provided a well-organized framework within which the officers could articulate their discontent and, in the long run, find a political voice and sense of personal and professional mission.

FREE OFFICERS

In post-war Egypt violence — assassinations, acts of sabotage and terror, riots, strikes and unruly demonstrations — characterized political life. The murder of Prime Minister Ahmad Mahir, in February 1945, inaugurated a rise in turmoil that would last until the Free Officers take-over. Mahir succeeded to office in October 1944, when Farouk dismissed the Wafdist leader Mustafa al-Nahhas, who for nearly three years had managed to avoid declaring war. With the war nearly over, that task fell to Mahir, but as he left parliament following his speech he was shot. Minority politicians tried, and failed, to renegotiate Egypt's relationship with Great Britain until in 1947 Britain agreed to withdraw its armed forces to its Suez Canal bases — but this no longer appeased the nationalists.

In the post-war economic slump, social upheaval threatened to engulf the country. The Second World War had been a powerful economic stimulant to a growing industrial base (more so than World War One) but the cost of living had nearly tripled between 1939 and 1945. Distribution of income remained highly skewed. Despite government efforts to curb inflation, "the enormous incidence of poverty persisted and may even have worsened." The industrial workforce, which by 1950 was greater than one million laborers, grew increasingly restive. A series of strikes and sit-ins in 1946–47 paralyzed textiles, Egypt's largest industry. Government forces turned the factory complexes north of Cairo at Shubra al-Khayma into a "veritable armed camp." [5] Workers joined forces with student activists in a series of political coalitions but, more importantly, in regular joint demonstrations that became more and more violent. On 9 February 1946, in an infamous incident marked in later years as a national day, during a student march from Cairo University toward parliament the police lifted the Abbas drawbridge across the Nile, resulting in the death of some twenty protesters. Two weeks later, when demonstrating students and workers stormed the British barracks, troops opened fire, killing twenty-three and wounding one hundred and twenty.

Although the countryside remained quiet, advocates of social reform increasingly turned turned attention toward the inequities in rural landholding. In the late 1940s, some twelve thousand families owned thirty-five percent of Egypt's arable land, with fewer than two thousand owning estates of two hundred feddans or more. At the other end of the social spectrum, thirty-five percent of the land was shared by two and a half million families, holding five feddans or less. It was estimated that only half of Egypt's landholders could live on what they grew, while 1.6 million families, sixty percent of the rural population, were landless. In the late forties, many industrial-

[5] Robert L. Tignor, *State, Private Enterprise and Economic Change in Egypt: 1918–1952* (Princeton: Princeton University Press, 1984), pp. 216, 221.

ists and leading merchants argued that agriculture was taxed too lightly. The reformers proposed a variety of schemes for land redistribution and advocated caps on the amount of land that could be legally owned.

As governments rose and fell with ever-greater rapidity and each new administration cleansed the house anew with self-righteous indignation, the country seemed to hover on the brink of collapse. For many, political corruption was encapsulated in the cynical catchphrase *hizbiyya* – fractious party politics at its worst. The Muslim Brotherhood, which had once toyed with the idea of opting into the political process, fell under the sway of their secret paramilitary wing. A self-styled Wafdist Vanguard composed primarily of young party adherents frustrated with their elders, the growing influence of conservative landed élite and the expulsion or angry resignations of reformers, struggled to push the majority party to the left. Communist movements, small, splintered but ideologically influential, began to galvanize industrial workers and students. State authorities failed to keep the peace; growing public dissatisfaction, fueled by stringent authoritarian measures and a declining economy, produced "a common disdain for law and order... a rationale for violence which hastened the end of Egypt's parliamentary life."[6] "Revolution-Revolution-Revolution," screamed a banner headline in the weekly paper of the Egyptian Socialist Party, an outgrowth of Young Egypt, the movement that had galvanized Nasser in the 1930s.

Against this backdrop, sometime in 1949, Nasser and his closest comrades founded a secret organization of "Free Officers," resolved to insulate themselves from civilian politics and explore their destiny as patriotic soldiers. Two crucial developments underscored this resolve. The first was Egypt's disastrous involvement in the 1948 Palestine War, a conflict

---

[6] Richard P. Mitchell, *The Society of the Muslim Brothers* (London: Oxford University Press, 1969), p. 313.

endorsed half-heartedly and at the last minute by the government, which proved a crucible for many who led units into
battle. The second was the subsequent government crackdown on opposition movements, particularly the Muslim
Brotherhood but also communist movements, with which
many of Nasser's circle had been, or were, affiliated. The war
they fought beyond Egypt's eastern border convinced the
Free Officers that they should enter the political fray back
home and the assault on the Brotherhood accentuated fears
of becoming embroiled in the political battles being fought
in the streets.

Egypt entered the Palestine conflict with neither military
preparation nor decisive political will; the combination proved
disastrous. Public opinion had become increasingly sympathetic
to the plight of Palestine's Arab population during the late
1930s, particularly during the ill-fated Arab rebellion of 1936–
39. Zionist groups, although representing a scant minority of
Egyptian Jews, continued to flourish openly. Even after agents
of the future Israeli Prime Minister Yitzhak Shamir's Stern
Gang assassinated the British Resident Minister Lord Moyne,
in November 1944 in the Cairo garden district of Zamalek,
high society remained undeterred. When a South African intelligence officer, Aubrey Eban – the future Israeli diplomat, Abba
Eban – married a Cairo socialite in 1945, also in Zamalek, the
guest list included, as well as the cream of Egyptian society, two
distinguished Zionist guests from Palestine: David Ben-Gurion
and future Mayor of Jerusalem Teddy Kollek.

However, by the late 1940s, the mood had shifted. Jewish
businesses and property became targets of mob violence.
The November 1947 United Nations resolution partitioning
Palestine into Zionist and Arab states came on the heels of the
Security Council's rejection of Egyptian complaints earlier that
autumn. As host country to the newly formed Arab League,
Egypt could not ignore calls to muster a "liberation army,"
especially as partition sparked a vicious civil war as Zionist and
Palestinian armed forces fought to maximize their territory

before Britain's scheduled withdrawal in May 1948. Students took to the streets, calling upon Prime Minister Mahmud al-Nuqrashi to arm them and send them into battle.

While Egypt's high command worried about the army's preparedness, political leaders encouraged the formation of paramilitary units. The Muslim Brotherhood rallied to the call; the military allowed officers temporarily to resign their commission and join the battle. Nasser reportedly sought a waiver but his request was rejected, presumably due to his teaching assignment in the military academy (although some suggest that his political activities had already drawn untoward attention). Others in his circle departed: Hasan Ibrahim and Abd al-Latif al-Baghdadi for Damascus and Kamal al-Din Husayn for Hebron. Within weeks, the situation changed dramatically. Prime Minister Nuqrashi, heeding the advice of his more cautious commanders, at first rejected the formal entry of his country into the conflict; but with other Arab states committing to enter after Britain's departure, and under pressure from the palace, Nuqrashi suddenly reversed his decision. On 16 May, a day after the Zionist declaration of Israeli statehood, Egyptian forces hastily mobilized for invasion via Gaza. Nasser, Abd al-Hakim Amr and Zakariya Muhyi al-Din found themselves traveling together by train to join their units.

Nasser's personal experiences, which he later described in his manifesto, *The Philosophy of the Revolution*, were emblematic of the Egyptian Palestine War narrative, marked by individual heroics undone by organizational ineptitude and political treachery. Unit commanders found themselves under-equipped, with sub-grade armaments and without adequate rations or supply lines. Nasser had to purchase provisions for his unit from local merchants. Officers listened bitterly to state radio broadcasts describing fictitious victories while they criticized their deployment orders which, they complained, had been designed to increase political visibility; they spread the units too thinly, at the expense of efficient offensive mobility. While briefly in hospital after sustaining a slight wound, Nasser observed at first-hand the inefficiency of rearguard support services. As weapons jammed or backfired, rumors proliferated that the King and chief ministers had sold Egypt's best equipment on the international arms market and pock-eted the profits. The press picked up the story of the "corrupt armaments," sparking a major scandal. The stories were later disproved but popular belief in their veracity reified them and they became a key component of Nasserist official history.

The archetypical moment of the official history is the mar-tyrdom of Lieutenant Ahmad Abd al-Aziz. The commander of Egyptian volunteer forces in Palestine, Abd al-Aziz was wounded by friendly fire outside Jerusalem in August 1948 and died in the company of Kamal al-Din Husayn, a Free Officer founder. His dying words, urging his comrades to carry their struggle back to the home front, where the "real battle" awaited them, were canonized, primarily via Nasser's published account. Nasser later recalled his own thoughts, while under siege at Falluja, a vital crossroads in the northern Negev, where he had been posted after a brief home leave during the July–October 1948 ceasefire. When the ceasefire collapsed in mid-October, the "Falluja brigade" found itself engaged in heavy fighting, then surrounded by enemy forces. "We have been duped – pushed into a battle for which we were unprepared. Vile ambitions, insidious intrigues and inordinate lusts are toying with our destinies and we are left here under fire unarmed." Egypt, Nasser reflected, constituted "a second Falluja, on a larger scale."[7]

Nasser took part in talks with Israeli officers, several of whom, including Yigal Allon, later Israeli Foreign Minister, remembered him as charismatic. Rejecting calls to surrender, the brigade remained immobile throughout the winter, until Egypt signed an armistice under the United Nations' auspices

----

[7] Gamal Abdel-Nasser, *Egypt's liberation: The philosophy of the revolution* (Washington, DC: Public Affairs Press, 1955), pp. 13–14.

in February 1949. The Israelis allowed the besieged units to march home carrying their arms and with colors flying.

Not unlike other soldiers who have fought bravely for losing causes, the heroes of Falluja received an ambivalent reception. With a continuing parliamentary investigation into the charges of war profiteering, many leading politicians wished they would return quietly to their barracks. Ignoring official advice, Um Kulthum, the most popular singer in the Arab world, insisted on throwing a fête for the Falluja heroes. Photos snapped during the party show the officers grinning broadly, toasting and being toasted by a superstar whose music they adored. The moment, though short-lived, was surely a bit intoxicating for some, who would later revel in close associations with music and film stars. Nasser and his circle, more than ever committed to playing some role in the national debate about Egypt's future, returned to an very volatile situation.

Political violence spiked in the late 1940s. The Muslim Brotherhood engaged in a dangerous confrontation with government forces and, in December 1948, the Prime Minister outlawed the movement. Several days later, a young Brother disguised as a police officer shot Nuqrashi dead outside the interior ministry. Nuqrashi's successor, Ibrahim Abd al-Hadi, cracked down hard on all political opponents. In February 1949, in downtown Cairo, police agents gunned down the Brotherhood's founder and Supreme Guide, Hasan al-Banna. Sometime later, Nasser was summoned to a meeting with the Prime Minister, who chastised him for his political proclivities. Nasser kept his cool, denying the charges levied against him. He received only a verbal reprimand but the incident must have shaken him. With the Muslim Brotherhood in government sights and a state of disarray – the paramilitary secret organization had by now become virtually autonomous – Nasser and his closest collaborators decided that distance would serve them best.

The Free Officers coalesced into a formal secret society, resolved to organize independently of all civilian-based political opposition movements, regardless of ideological affinity. In

the autumn of 1949 Nasser, four comrades from his Muslim
Brotherhood cell and three other close colleagues formed an
executive committee, with Nasser as its chief. These members
represented diverse political orientations but viewed themselves first and foremost as military men and organized their
movement around military affiliation. By the time they moved,
in July 1952, the executive committee included at least one
member from each major corps except the navy. Academy
instructors and unit commanders sought out like-minded
comrades, who rarely knew who were the movement's leaders.
Husayn al-Shafi`i remembers how, one morning in September
1951, Nasser, who he had known since the mid-1940s, stopped
at his office for what seemed an impromptu chat. That afternoon, several Free Officer insiders invited Shafi`i to join the
executive committee. The fluidity of this organizational plan
remained strong until the coup. Zakariya Muhyi al-Din, who
drew up the plan of action and shortly after joined the ruling
junta, claimed ignorance of the existence of a formal executive. For the time being, the Free Officers met in each others'
homes. The height of their overt politicking was a series of
leaflets – many of which were later reproduced for broader
public consumption – that called upon the "peoples' army" to
stand steadfast in the twin struggles against imperialism and
political corruption.

Friendships and collaboration with civilian and military
contemporaries from other opposition movements continued.
Relations with the left grew particularly close. Left-wing ideologues played an increasingly influential role in the thinking
of Nasser and his closest associates, even if many, like Nasser,
never accepted Marxist doctrine. The Free Officers printed
their leaflets on equipment owned by Haditu (the acronym
for the *Democratic Movement for National Liberation*, sometimes
referred to as DMNL in English-language literature), the largest communist front. Haditu members called Nasser by his
code name, Maurice. Relations were more complex with the
Muslim Brotherhood, who tended to view the movement as

an organizational offshoot. In early 1952, Abd al-Mun'im Abd al-Ra'uf, one of the Free Officers' founders, was expelled after questions of his primary loyalty, but channels remained open. The Brothers, like Haditu, were brought in for the last phases of planning the coup and leaders of both movements agreed to play subsidiary operational roles.

NEW ERA

The *coup d'état* of 23 July 1952 marked an accelerated decline of faith in the liberal order, as events spun out of control in the early 1950s. In late 1949, the King called for general elections; in January 1950 the Wafd swept to power with what appeared to be a truly reformist agenda, spearheaded by key cabinet appointments of younger, fresher faces, professionals with no deep party connections. The top positions, none the less, remained in the hands of party elders who, from Prime Minster Nahhas down, appeared unwilling or unable to curb party patronage or promote real change. Party politics reigned supreme, as promising ministers quit or lost their portfolios. Progressive intellectuals decried a "country of failure"; many soon began to articulate the need for a "just tyrant" to straighten out the mess.[8] In October 1951, in a last-ditch effort to rally the nation and while the King was on a European pleasure jaunt, Nahhas tore up the 1936 Anglo-Egyptian treaty that he had signed fifteen years earlier. The government now supported, through devious routes, the "popular struggle" against British forces in the Suez Canal Zone. Daily incidents of sniping and sabotage escalated and Britain lost patience. A one-sided battle, fought against Egyptian police and irregulars in Ismailia on 25 January 1952, enraged the home front. The

[8] Joel Gordon, *Nasser's blessed movement: Egypt's Free Officers and the July revolution* (New York and Oxford: Oxford University Press, 1992), pp. 25, 33.

next day – "Black Saturday" in Egyptian historiography – mobs, perhaps fueled by spontaneous combustion, but surely steered by *agents provocateurs* – burned foreign or foreign-associated businesses and clubs in Cairo. The government responded slowly and Farouk, who had been celebrating the birth of his heir in the nearby Abdin Palace, sacked Nahhas. A new minority prime minister declared martial law. For six months Egypt tottered. Three prime ministers failed to deliver promises either to purge the political order or talk the British out of their Canal bases.

The Free Officers initially supported the government's abrogation of the 1936 treaty and fought alongside the irregulars, but they decried its unwillingness to declare all-out war against the British. With a heightened animosity against "traitors" in the high command, they ran opposition candidates, led by General Muhammad Nagib, the only senior commander to emerge from Palestine a hero. The dissidents won control of the Officers Club governing board. The high command took notice but failed to grasp the significance of the power-play. The Free Officers (for the first time) discussed a *coup d'état* but acted decisively only when, in mid-July, civilian contacts warned them of imminent arrests. Springing into action, a small group drafted a set of orders to call units into the streets of Cairo and Alexandria. The Muslim Brotherhood agreed to cut off any British intervention from the Canal Zone, a response that never materialized. Despite a series of errors – lead units rolled toward general headquarters an hour early, Nasser and Amr, monitoring activities in a private car, were detained briefly by their own operatives, Sadat, hastily recalled from El Arish, either never having received clear orders or seeking to camouflage his participation in the operation, went to the cinema and missed zero hour – the rebels arrested the high command, secured key installations in Cairo and blockaded Farouk in his Alexandria palace with no loss of life on either side and only scattered casualties. (Two soldiers later died in a brief exchange of gunfire outside Ras al-Tin Palace on 26 July.) On 23 July, Egyptians woke to a message from a new general command informing them that the nation was in safe hands and that a new era, guided by "sound" democratic principles, was beginning.

During the following few days the Free Officers set the tone they hoped would resonate throughout the country. They abolished titles, stripped government ministers of private vehicles and appointed a civilian prime minister, Ali Mahir, a man with troubling palace connections but of recognized honesty. On 26 July, they exiled Farouk without trial and with a modicum of formality. The Free Officers executive, expanded to fourteen members to include key operational leaders and several popular commanders, voted on all actions but Nasser stood

Free Officers. Leaders of the July 1952 Free Officers *coup*, visibly tired, sitting in General Headquarters within hours of seizing power. Muhammad Nagib sits behind the desk, but the camera is centered on Nasser. Abd al-Hakim Amr stands directly to Nasser's left. Anwar al-Sadat sits toward the back, sporting a tie, to Nasser's right. (Property of the author.)

behind all decisions and restrained fellow officers who sought
to exact more draconian measures, such as trying and perhaps
executing the monarch.

One tragic incident stained the peaceful transition of power,
prompting the ruling junta, as a collective, to flex their muscles
and assert martial power. In early August, within three weeks
of their takeover, workers struck at a textile plant in the mill
town of Kafr al-Dawwar. Locked in a bitter conflict with management over the right to organize, the workers, convinced
that the new regime would sympathize with their demands,
marched, shouting slogans praising the officers. On the night
of 12 August, things turned violent. Troops were mobilized
to restore order but in the ensuing clashes four workers, two
soldiers and one policeman lost their lives. In the aftermath, a
special military tribunal sentenced two workers to hang. Nasser
reportedly objected to the harsh sentences but allowed himself
to be outvoted. The two workers were executed on 7 September, an action that poisoned relations between communist
movements – and leftists in general – and the new regime.

For their official front man, the Free Officers turned to General Nagib, a recognized public figure with a congenial visage,
high rank and advanced years. Muhammad Nagib, who briefly
served as Egypt's first republican president, lent the "Blessed
Movement" (for the first six months of their rule they did not
call themselves a revolutionary command) a degree of respect-
ability and breathing room while the officers considered their
future steps. Nagib's credibility proved instrumental when, in
early September, the officers dismissed Ali Mahir, appointed the
General in his place and pushed through a land reform that large
owners had opposed. The measure limited family landholding
to two hundred feddans. In its initial phase, some 1700 land-
owners, 425 of them members of the royal family, lost approximately 657,000 feddans, one-tenth of Egypt's arable land.

In January 1953, six months after seizing power and impatient with the reluctance of the political parties to purge their
ranks, the officers outlawed political parties, decreed a three-

year "transition period" of martial rule and instituted the first
of a series of show trials. Overnight, their movement became
a "revolution" and the ruling junta the Revolutionary Command Council (RCC). In June 1953, they proclaimed Egypt a
republic and appointed Muhammad Nagib president. Despite
the growing alienation of leftist forces and a falling out with
the Muslim Brotherhood – who had not been outlawed in
January – the officers retained a reservoir of popular support.
By late 1953, the show trials had began to backfire and British
recalcitrance, even in the face of continued guerilla activity
and growing American pressure to resolve the issue of the
Suez bases, began to erode their popularity. The interior strains
became accentuated when Nagib began to act with greater
autonomy from the RCC.

In March 1954, the officers faced the most dangerous
challenge to their authority. In January, after disturbances on
university campuses, the RCC had ordered scores of Muslim
Brothers to be arrested. In late February, without warning, they
stunned the nation by announcing the dismissal of Muhammad
Nagib. Then, in the face of a wave of popular discontent they
agreed, cautiously, to loosen restrictions on assembly and
media censorship. Suddenly, they were faced with widespread
calls in the streets and the press for them to return to the barracks and leave politics to the politicians. In a risky gambit, the
officers announced their resignation then, following a spate
of rowdy demonstrations and strikes – some of them clearly
staged – retracted their decision. In the following months
the regime consolidated its power and purged labor unions,
professional organizations, the universities, the press and the
military – including a number of fellow conspirators who had
stood against them in March. Muhammad Nagib resumed his
position as president but in November 1954 the RCC placed
him under house arrest, where he remained until 1971.

By the end of the "March crisis" Gamal Abd al-Nasser had
clearly emerged to the public eye as the revolution's real leader.
During the previous two years he had shared the spotlight with

other colleagues, some of whom, like the outgoing Salah Salim, appeared far more comfortable in front of the camera. After March 1954, Nasser became prime minister. He appeared frequently in the press and was caricatured on the cover of popular picture magazines as the personification of the new Egypt: pyramid builder, armor-shield against reactionary terror, football hero. If many, perhaps most, Egyptians still feared him as a stern and taciturn figure, that began to change after his regime negotiated Britain's total withdrawal from Egyptian soil and he delivered a stirring national address, punctuated by the sounds of an assassin's misfired bullets.

The moment was 24 October 1954; the site, Manshiya Square in Alexandria. Nasser was uncomfortable speaking in public; he had done much better around a table with Anthony Nutting, Britain's chief negotiator. In telegraphs, Nutting described Egypt's new leader as a sincere, personally honest, patriot. As he stood at the rostrum under the night sky, Nasser began haltingly, parroting stock phrases about independence and national pride. After several minutes he shifted gears, speaking emotionally, if still stiffly, of his joy at standing in the very square where, in 1930, he had first demonstrated against British rule. Five minutes into his speech, eight shots rang out. For an instant, silence prevailed then, as if transformed (skeptics still claim the entire affair was orchestrated but the speaker's emotional mixture of panic and courage seems spontaneous) Nasser delivered his first, great, unscripted public address. For nearly ten minutes, broken only by a praise chanter's call to the crowd – "God be with you, Gamal" – an impassioned, nearly hysterical Nasser swore to live and die for his country: "I am Gamal Abd al-Nasser, of you and for you ... I will live until I die for your sake, on behalf of you and on behalf of your freedom and your honor ...." Then came the phrase that is most remembered: "If Gamal Abd al-Nasser should die, I will not die – for all of you are Gamal Abd al-Nasser – Egypt's well-being is linked not to Gamal Abd al-Nasser but to you and your struggle."

The assailant proved to be a member of the Muslim Brotherhood. How high up the chain of command the plot to kill Nasser had been approved is still controversial but it seems clear that the Supreme Guide, Hasan al-Hudaybi, had been present when his paramilitary chiefs and guidance council members discussed the possibility. In the immediate aftermath of the assassination attempt, the regime set out to destroy the Brotherhood, arresting thousands of suspected members and establishing a special military tribunal to try the movement's leaders. In December 1954, in a dramatic series of hearings supervised by Anwar al-Sadat, the assailant and five Brotherhood leaders (although not Hudaybi) went to the gallows. Sadat threatened bloodshed if Egyptians continued to oppose what had been a peaceful, "white" revolution. However, the battle had been fought and won and the enemies chased down and imprisoned. Popular sentiment, encouraged by the regime's propaganda, looked to a courageous and suddenly charismatic leader.

The persona would grow with time. Gamal. Mister President. *Rayyis.* Even his wife called him that. One might see the leader driving himself through the streets, or approach him at the cinema to greet or share a personal grievance. A simple man of simple tastes, who loved nothing better than a peasant meal of cheese, bread and olives and who only begrudgingly built an extension to his modest home to accommodate his growing family (by 1955 he and Tahiya had five children — Hoda and Mona were followed by three boys — Khalid, Abd al-Hamid and Abd al-Hakim). In 1954, he published his personal manifesto, *The Philosophy of the Revolution*, which became an authoritative account of the Free Officers rise to power and Nasser's personal imprint on the movement. Readers around the world were introduced to the young patriot's political education in the streets, barracks and battlefields and his vision of a dramatic leadership role for Egypt in the overlapping Arab, African and Muslim spheres. The text is romantic; some say naïve but to Britain's ambassador in Cairo it reflected a "breadth of vision, humanity and idealism." His American counterpart judged Nasser "selfless and icily intelligent," an authoritarian but honest leader of "uncompromising realism."[9]

Nasser's close colleagues observed his rise with respect but no small amount of personal hurt. He had always been first among equals, convincing others to follow his lead more by force of personality than coercion. Yet now he kept a greater distance from most of his oldest comrades. When the revolutionary command proved impotent during the March crisis and many of its members torn by self-doubt, he had worked beyond their purview, with a small clique of second-tier officers, some of whom would soon become his closest advisors. He now looked toward disbanding the RCC and replacing it with a formal civilian cabinet. Khalid Muhyi al-Din, one of his closest army comrades, fell from grace during the March crisis. In early 1955, when he returned from a punitive posting abroad to sit again around the executive command table, he recalls he was stunned to see the others jump to attention when Nasser entered and refer to him deferentially, by title. When Nasser mounted a rostrum at ceremonies to mark the third anniversary of the Revolution in July 1955, he failed to ask his comrades, sitting beside him, to stand for the crowd's approbation.

A month earlier, on 25 June, the masses had approved, by popular referendum, a new constitution and elected Nasser president of the republic. "We're the people," sang Abd al-Halim Hafiz for the occasion:

> You who stay awake nights so that our glorious sun will rise,
> We are your soldiers. Take us by the hand, Egypt trusts in you.
> Tomorrow our country will be a paradise and you will be with us.
> For we have chosen you and will march in your footsteps …

Not everyone joined the procession. The Muslim Brothers – in prison, exile or hiding – had waged war on the regime

[9] Joel Gordon, *Nasser's blessed movement: Egypt's Free Officers and the July revolution* (New York and Oxford: Oxford University Press, 1992), pp. 172, 188.

and lost. Communists, many also now incarcerated, expressed disappointment at the limits on social reform and the regime's willingness to talk with the Americans, especially with regard to restricting left-wing political activity. Old-guard party bosses had been stripped of their livelihoods and political rights. Younger party loyalists had grown wary of the officers' authoritarian tendencies. But for the majority, cynical, dispirited Egypt had found a new hero. Nasser had discovered his role.

THE GREATER NATION:
1956–1961

> Beloved nation, the greater nation,
> Day after day, its glory increases,
> Its victories, fulfilling its life.
> My nation grows and becomes liberated ...
> [*Al-Watan al-akbar* (The Greater Nation), 1961]

By 1956, Nasser's face was well known throughout the world, gracing the covers of foreign magazines and newspapers. In late 1954, in the American heartland, *The Milwaukee Journal* headlined his achievements. By the next year his *Philosophy of the Revolution* was translated into English. He published policy statements in *Foreign Affairs* and gave interviews to leading print and broadcast journalists. Following his very visible attendance of the Bandung Conference of Non-aligned Nations, held in Indonesia in April 1955, Nasser's reputation soared as he rubbed shoulders with Sukarno, Nehru, Tito and Zhou Enlai.

In February 1956 he spoke to Howard K. Smith of CBS Radio. Smith asked Nasser to assure American listeners that his was a "constructive, sincere revolution" rather than "just one more nationalistic dictatorship, as your critics maintain." In clearly enunciated, fluid English, Nasser outlined the revolution's *Six Principles*: anti-colonialism, anti-feudalism, anti-corruption, social justice, the creation of a strong national army and clean democracy, not, as he put it, the "game of democracy" that had plagued the old regime. He praised the evacuation accord reached with the British in October 1954, scheduled to happen in June 1956. Land reform, he asserted, had broken the backs of the feudalists and spearheaded the drive toward a more equitable society. A "political vacuum" still prevailed but the 1956 constitution would fortify a new democratic order. Egypt needed a strong army, not to carve out an Arab empire but to defend itself, most immediately from Israel. To that end, his government had been forced to turn to the Soviet bloc for help.

In 1956, Nasser's Egypt was on the threshold of a new chapter. The regime's early, vague aims, drafted by conspiratorial officers and later codified as the *raison d'etre* for political and social revolution, remained in place as the regime consolidated its power. Before 1955, Nasser and his comrades could afford only (indeed were compelled) to look inward. The social revolution at home – the pursuit of "sound" democracy and greater equity – remained vital to their sense of self. However, their very success in consolidating their authority at home thrust them suddenly into the forefront of regional and world affairs, which would come to dominate their attention and threaten to impede or undo much of what they hoped to achieve.

GAZA AND SUEZ

In early February 1955, Ihsan Abd al-Quddus, editor of the influential weekly *Ruz al-Yusuf*, noted in his leader column that foreign affairs would dominate the next phase of the Free Officers revolution. An insider, who had called for the collective resignation of the RCC in March 1954 and wound up in prison, he could not have been more prescient. The home front was stabilized, pacified and won over and Egypt needed to look outward to fortify its position. Britain had finally agreed to leave, with a degree of begrudging respect and hopes for an ongoing, if redefined, defense relationship. However, regional and cold war rivalries suddenly made the attainment of independence complex. Nasser had outlined three broad themes for Egyptian involvement in foreign affairs and he now took Egypt headlong into the fray.

Egypt's "positive neutrality" – the desire to avoid unilateral alignment with either the Western or Soviet blocs – reflected an ideological yearning that proved untenable in a bi-polar superpower world. "Pacto-mania" ruled and, since Egypt remained linked to Britain and had found a supportive friend in the United States, it seemed to policymakers in London and Washington that Nasser would naturally bring his country into a pro-Western security alliance. The British Prime Minister, Anthony Eden, led a delegation to Cairo in February 1955 (while *en route* to Bangkok for a meeting of SEATO, the South East Asian Treaty Organization) but failed to recruit Egypt into a proposed Baghdad Pact of Middle Eastern nations. American pressure followed. Obsessed with what they felt to be the Soviet threat to the region, neither London nor Washington understood the degree to which Nasser's reluctance expressed honest trepidation at lingering imperialist ambitions among the old colonial powers. Egyptian officials expressed their wariness in idiomatic terms: if the colonial powers left through the front door they should not be allowed to sneak back in through an open window.

Meetings between Western and Egyptian officials, some at the highest levels, produced what appeared to American and British participants to be a series of understandings about Egypt's place in the Cold War world order. In meetings with Eden and others, Nasser claimed to sympathize with Western aspirations. Yet, in the Arab world, especially in speeches and radio broadcasts, Egypt's leaders denounced the Baghdad Pact as a neo-colonial venture. In early 1955, when Pakistan, Iran and the pro-British Iraqi regime signed the pact, the Egyptians unleashed a major propaganda campaign, directed at Jordan, Syria and Lebanon that ultimately proved successful in confining the Baghdad Pact to the "northern tier" of the Middle East and thus rendering it tangential to central Arab affairs.

Egypt was accused of fomenting disturbances and plotting to undermine regimes throughout the Arab world. Nasser's regime, sometimes with the Saudis (although this story remains sketchy at best), subsidized opposition activities in neighboring countries, often through military attachés working with state security. However, Nasser's greatest influence was overt yet indirect, the result of public statements and a wide-ranging media blitz through the newly established *Sawt al-Arab* (Voice of the Arabs) radio station, which publicized the liberation strug-

Voice of the Arabs. The Radio and Television Building, nerve center for Egyptian artistic and political broadcasts throughout the Middle East and the broader decolonizing world. (Photograph by the author.)

gles of colonized and newly independent peoples and broadcast news reports and calls to arms in Arabic and, eventually, many Afro-Asian languages. Nasser was vilified in London and Paris (where Egypt's support for the Algerian independence struggle had incensed the French leadership) and his American friends, although they never broke with him entirely, came to see his policies as inimical to Western interests. The warm greeting he received from the Chinese Premier, Zhou Enlai, in Bandung underscored the dangers of neutrality and heightened questions as to whether he represented friend or foe.

The escalation of the conflict between Israel and its Arab neighbors ultimately pushed Nasser into the Soviet camp. Following the 1949 armistice agreement that ended the Palestine War, Egypt and Israel worked behind the scenes to police their borders – even patrolling together – and engaged in discussions aimed at formalizing relations. With only one unit stationed in the Gaza strip, the Egyptians could not prevent dispossessed Palestinians and Bedouin from crossing into Israel – something which happened far more often for economic and social reasons (such as to reclaim possessions or crops, cultivate or graze former lands or visit relatives) than to strike at an enemy. Organized gangs engaged in cross-border smuggling. A series of Israeli retaliatory raids in late 1951 and early 1952 prompted the Egyptians to crack down on border crossings. The Free Officers did nothing to change Egyptian policy after their takeover and even increased their efforts to police the frontier. The general atmosphere grew increasingly poisoned, as violence grew on other fronts. In August 1953, an Israeli raid on the Jordanian village of Qibya, undertaken by Ariel Sharon's notorious Unit 101, left forty-three Jordanian soldiers and sixty-nine civilians dead in what many considered a deliberate atrocity.

Things fell apart in late 1954, just as Egypt mended relations with the British and Nasser emerged as the man in charge. In October 1954, Egyptian police arrested eleven Egyptian Jews and two Israelis implicated in a series of bombings and attempted bombings the previous July. The Egyptians had been recruited several years earlier by a Mossad operative, who had entered the country on a British passport. Wary of the close ties between the Free Officers regime and the Americans, and fearing the regional implications of the impending Anglo-Egyptian evacuation accord (Heads of Agreement were approved in July and the final accord signed in October), in particular the absence of a foreign-occupied buffer zone and the possibility of Britain turning arms over to the Egyptians, Israeli intelligence authorized covert action to sabotage Anglo-Egyptian and Egyptian-American relations by undermining confidence in the regime's ability to protect foreign interests and maintain civil order. On 2 July, several letter bombs exploded in the main Alexandria post office; two weeks later the American libraries in Cairo and Alexandria were targeted. None of the explosions caused serious damage. On 23 July, Revolution Day, a saboteur was caught outside an Alexandria cinema when the explosives he was carrying ignited prematurely. Plans to turn the national "festivities into a day of mourning"[1] by setting off devices in four cinemas (and presumably laying the blame on the Muslim Brotherhood) led instead to the discovery of secret arms caches and the eventual arrest of the entire circle of conspirators.

Operation Suzannah, referred to in official Israeli circles as "the mishap" – and later, after the defense minister who reaped the blame, the "Lavon Affair" – was not approved at cabinet level and was initiated without the knowledge of the Prime Minister, Moshe Sharett. The operation failed in all respects and hastened the deterioration of Israeli-Egyptian relations. From the summer of 1954, Nasser and other regime officials began denouncing the "Zionist enemy" with increasing regularity in public speeches and editorials. In September 1954, with the final stages of Anglo-Egyptian negotiations underway, Israel dispatched a freighter, the *Bat Galim*, to attempt a passage

---

[1] Michael M. Laskier, *The Jews of Egypt: 1920–1970* (New York: NYU Press, 1992), p. 210.

through the Suez Canal, hoping to provoke an international judgement before the withdrawal of British forces. Since the 1949 armistice ending the Palestine War, Egypt had denied Israeli shipping or ships bound for Israel the right of transit, arguing that the state of war superseded the rights accorded to other nations under the international convention which governed the Canal. Unofficially, the Nasser regime turned a blind eye to shipping it considered non-aggressive but the Egyptians could not ignore this deliberate challenge.

Egyptian authorities impounded the freighter. The UN Security Council agreed to take up the case but before its meeting the Egyptians freed the crew and offered to release the ship and its cargo to third-party representatives so long as it did not repeat its attempt to enter the Canal. In December the thirteen saboteurs were tried, attracting international attention. In January 1955, despite persistent lobbying from world Zionist leaders and sympathizers, the Egyptians executed two of the convicted Israeli spies (two of the thirteen had been acquitted; one had committed suicide). Nasser supposedly promised leniency but colleagues persuaded him that to favor Zionist agents, while executing Muslim Brotherhood leaders, would be politically incendiary.

The border fires continued to smolder. Israeli leaders complained of incursions by Egyptian intelligence, some of which resulted in fighting. Nasser, somewhat injudiciously, blamed renegade elements, including the Muslim Brotherhood. The Israeli Prime Minister, Sharett, who had looked forward to American-sponsored negotiations with the Egyptians, was compelled to bring the hard-liner David Ben-Gurion into his cabinet as defense minister. Six days later, on 28 February 1955, Israel staged a major incursion into Gaza. In the bloodiest engagement between the two nations since the Palestine War, Israeli forces killed thirty-one Egyptians, most of them soldiers. The Gaza raid was a turning point in Israeli-Egyptian relations. Rather than curb cross-border encroachments, which had remained either local or aimed at intelligence gathering,

"Operation Black Arrow" destroyed any hopes for a rapprochement: "In effect, the two states stopped toying with the possibility of a settlement and plunged headlong down the road to war."[2]

During the year, a series of military engagements, the most violent occurring on Egyptian soil, pushed the two countries to the brink. Egypt's leaders, confronted with their inability to defend their country and worried by Israeli boasts that Cairo was within four days march, increased their search for sophisticated armaments. As the situation deteriorated on the Egyptian-Israeli border, Nasser came under pressure from his military commanders. In the immediate aftermath of the Gaza raid, the Egyptian military began arming and training Palestinian *fidayin* (commandos), who undertook a series of raids into Israel. In August 1955, the Israelis occupied sections of the demilitarized zone along the truce lines and staged another major incursion into Gaza which left thirty-six Egyptians dead. Nasser unleashed the *fidayin* and tightened Egypt's blockade, (a legal, but diplomatically incendiary, act) over the Straits of Tiran, the route for ships to Israel's disputed port city, Eilat. Egyptian officials underscored the government's rejection of formal relations with Israel: Egypt would not initiate aggression but would "maintain a nonbelligerent state of war."[3] Ben-Gurion and his hawkish associates spoke forcefully about an inevitable pre-emptive war, to fortify Israel's position.

The arms race threatened to destabilize the entire region. When Western nations refused Egyptian entreaties, Nasser turned eastward. On 24 September 1955, after one final attempt to persuade the West, the Egyptians bought 200 million Egyptian pounds' worth of arms, ostensibly from the Czech government. Washington insiders did not see this as

---

[2] Benny Morris, *Israel's border wars, 1949–1956* (Oxford: Clarendon Press, 1997), p. 350.

[3] Keith Wheelock, *Nasser's new Egypt* (New York: Frederick A. Praeger, 1960), p. 234.

closing the door on future collaboration with Egypt, but Israeli leaders panicked at Egypt's sudden military parity and ability to hit targets inside Israel, especially from the air. In October, Ben-Gurion ordered military strategists to draft plans for the capture of the Tiran Straits. In November, two days after Ben-Gurion succeeded Sharett as Prime Minister, a major Israeli raid resulted in fifty Egyptian deaths. The Israelis concluded a major arms accord with the French government, which was already planned but now took on sudden urgency. Less concerned than the Americans or British to tie weapons sales to Arab-Israeli diplomatic initiatives, and incensed by Egyptian support for the Algerian liberation struggle, France became Israel's primary supplier. The French provided a second instalment in October 1956, just in time for the Suez War.

The deterioration of Egyptian-Israeli relations and Nasser's intransigence over the Baghdad Pact provide the context for the decision taken by American and British policymakers in the summer of 1956 to suspend the aid Egypt had been promised for the construction of a high dam at Aswan. Egypt had resisted certain terms of the loan, resentful of stipulations that bound them to reject bids from communist nations, undertake any new foreign obligations or borrow money without the approval of the World Bank. Despairing of losing the agreement (some say convinced he would) Nasser instructed his ambassador in Washington to accept, but to inform the American Secretary of State, John Foster Dulles, that Egypt also had a Soviet proposal in hand. When Dulles responded by withdrawing American assistance, Nasser retaliated dramatically.

On 26 July, in the same Alexandria square where he had survived the assassination attempt two years earlier, Nasser proclaimed the nationalization of the Suez Canal Company. It is unquestionably his greatest speech. For nearly half an hour, he described his recent meeting with non-aligned leaders in Yugoslavia and decried inequities in the treatment Egypt received from the Western powers, especially with regard to Israel. Suddenly, as he alluded to the visit of the President of the

World Bank, Eugene Black, Nasser found a historical analogy which struck a chord of Egyptian outrage. He felt, he said, as if he were speaking to Ferdinand de Lesseps. Nasser spoke the name of this French entrepreneur and Canal visionary some ten times in the next five minutes. It was more than a history lesson for, on hearing the name, a small team of technicians and intelligence agents moved to occupy key installations and seize company records. Fourteen minutes later, Nasser revealed to the rapturous assembly that Egypt had nationalized the Suez Canal Company. "We will build the high dam," he proclaimed. All over the country, Egyptians – sons and daughters of discredited pashas and displaced politicians, leftists and Islamists alike – poured into the streets to express their jubilation. Their cries echoed throughout the Arab world, far beyond Egypt.

From late July to early October Egyptian diplomats engaged in protracted discussions to defuse what had become an international crisis. In press interviews, Nasser endeavored to assure Canal users he would do nothing – to do anything would be suicidal, he asserted – to deny their right of passage. Sovereignty over the waterway was, the Egyptians insisted, guaranteed by the 1954 Anglo-Egyptian accord. Egypt promised to preserve the security and freedom of navigation provided in the 1888 international convention. In a personal telegram, Nasser explained to Nehru:

> Declared object of British occupation of canal zone was to
> ensure both and when they evacuated after Suez Base Treaty
> of 1954 they accepted that the guarantee by us in that treaty
> was enough and satisfactory. Disappearance of company, which
> would anyhow have happened in 1968, does not affect that
> guarantee and have reiterated it.[4]

Nasser and his top aides believed that the longer they avoided a confrontation, the easier it would be to see the crisis through

---

[4] Mohammed H. Heikal, *Cutting the lion's tail: Suez through Egyptian eyes* (London: Andre Deutsch, 1986), p. 141.

without violence. In a series of meetings in London, the Canal users drafted principles of understanding. Egyptian delegates attended the first round but after the insult handed to Egypt by a delegation to Cairo, headed by Australia's Prime Minister, Robert Menzies, they boycotted the second. When John Foster Dulles sensed that the Suez Canal Users Association, following Britain's lead, were seeking pretexts for war, he undermined the initiative, asserting that American shipping would sail round Africa rather than shoot its way through the Canal. The United Nations took up the matter, stalled, then seemed to have reached accord. Egyptian pilots and engineers, despite predictions of disaster, kept the Canal running smoothly. However, behind the scenes, high-level French, Israeli and British officials conspired to provoke a crisis which would validate reoccupation of the Canal Zone and bring down the Nasser regime.

The Suez War began on 29 October 1956, when Israeli forces, with no immediate provocation, drove suddenly into Egyptian territory, across the northern Sinai Peninsula toward the Canal and southward, to Sharm al-Sheikh. The Egyptians initially misread their predicament. "We have been monitoring closely what's going on and it looks to us as if all they want to do is to start up sandstorms in the desert," Nasser told Muhammad Hasanayn Haykal.[5] He, and his generals, viewed the assault either as a last-ditch Israeli effort to forestall the UN accord and prolong the crisis, a limited operation to occupy Gaza or even a diversionary action to draw attention away from a major assault on Jordan. The reality of the invasion, in scope and intent, quickly became clear.

The next day, Britain and France delivered an ultimatum to both sides to withdraw ten miles from the Canal on their respective banks. Israel, still advancing, agreed, while Egypt, with 30,000 troops engaged in combat in the Sinai, refused. The British and French then bombed Egyptian air bases, including some near Cairo, prompting Egypt to evacuate the Sinai.

[5] Heikal, *Cutting the lion's tail*, p. 177.

On 5 November, Anglo-French forces occupied Port Said and other Canal cities. Anthony Eden's "police action" looked to Egyptians (and much of the rest of the world) much like the second prong of a pre-arranged and orchestrated "tripartite aggression." Demonstrators took to the streets of London and the BBC refused government requests to deny the opposition airtime after Eden's televised address. Anthony Nutting, a minister of state, who had been involved in the conspiracy, resigned in protest, although without articulating his reasons.

With the Egyptian army beleaguered, despite spirited local resistance in Port Said, the future of the Nasser regime hung in the balance. Many, including Abd al-Hakim Amr, his closest comrade and commander of the armed forces, advocated surrender. Salah Salim, a Free Officers founder and RCC member, urged Nasser to turn himself over to the British authorities as a supreme act of personal sacrifice to the nation. However, the American president, Dwight Eisenhower, a week away from elections and outraged at a military action undertaken without American knowledge or approval, ordered the invasion to cease. He resorted to economic blackmail, openly threatening to undermine the British pound. Soviet intimations that they might unleash nuclear weapons against Western Europe if the invasion did not stop added to the crisis atmosphere. On 6–7 November the aggressors accepted a UN-mediated ceasefire. In late December, the Europeans pulled their forces out of Egypt. The Israelis, who had consolidated their domination of the Red Sea coast and retained their right to sail through the Straits of Tiran, withdrew from Sinai the following spring.

Suez ruined Anthony Eden's career, fueled the fires of the Arab-Israeli conflict and turned Gamal Abd al-Nasser into a regional superstar. The exposure of the conspiracy served to strengthen Nasser's claims to have defeated the forces of imperialism. Egypt's performance on the battlefield was irrelevant (except in retrospect, as none of its tactical failures were evaluated or addressed before the events of June 1967). Egypt suffered between one and three thousand battlefield deaths and five thousand soldiers were captured. Yet, the home front had stood firm and the people were steadfast. Refugees streaming westward from the Canal cities carried placards and adorned their vehicles with Nasser's portrait. Behind the scenes, he had assumed personal control of the war effort, ordering the air force to take refuge, the Sinai to be evacuated and the Canal to be blocked to further shipping. His address on 9 November, in a Friday sermon from the pulpit of the al-Azhar Mosque, the thousand-year-old center of Islamic learning in the heart of medieval Cairo, as bombs fell in the distance, resonated with the populace. The aggressors had agreed to withdraw but the battle against imperialism would continue and the world stood behind Egypt. "We will fight on and on," he concluded, "and never submit." It became the basis of a popular anthem penned by the multi-talented Salah Jahin:

> We'll fight on, we'll fight on – the people will all fight on.
> We're not afraid of those who advance.
> We'll fight on in millions – we'll fight on, until victory.
> Long live Egypt! Long live Egypt!
> [*Hanharib* (We'll Fight On), 1956]

Egyptians of the Suez generation still recall the conflict's other anthems with pride:

> Leave my skies be, the skies are aflame,
> Leave off my canal, the waters are gorged …
> This is my land, my father fell martyr here.
> And my father told us to tear our enemies to pieces.
> [*Du'a sima'i* (Leave My Skies), 1956]

> Oh, my weapon, it has been a long time – I miss you in my
>   struggle.
> Speak, I'm awake …
> The people are mountains, seas, a volcano of anger, ready to erupt.
> An earthquake that will cleave the earth to make their
>   [enemies'] graves.
> [*Wallahi zaman ya silahi* (Oh, My Weapon, It Has Been a Long
> Time), 1956]

Wherever Nasser went, the crowds mobbed him.

REMAKING EGYPT

Suez marked a major turning point in Egyptian and colonial history. In Britain, the "lion's last roar" heralded the end of empire. Anthony Eden, ill and in public disgrace, resigned in January 1957. Once a shining star of British politics, Winston Churchill's fair-haired heir, his downfall was his monomaniacal obsession with Nasser – in his mind, Hitler on the Nile – and an inability to read radical anti-colonial nationalism through any lens other than pre-war fascism. His successor, Harold Macmillan, dispensed with the rhetoric of "appeasement" and recognized the "winds of change" sweeping the colonial world. France, humiliated in Indochina, intensified its efforts to maintain sovereignty over Algeria, embarking on policies of concentration, bombing civilian targets and torture that would eventually spark a domestic crisis and calls for evacuation. Israel, despite being forced to withdraw from highly coveted territory in the Sinai Peninsula, reveled in the achievements of its armed forces and gained a new sense of regional security. Egypt agreed to allow UN forces to patrol the common border. Despite the remaining tensions, relations with its neighbors and the explosive growth of an impoverished Palestinian refugee population, the next Arab-Israeli war was a decade away.

After Suez, the Egyptian regime, seizing the upsurge of good will, looked inward to the consolidation of its national project. Islamist and Communist dissidents remained in prison – but the latter began to reorganize. Between 1957 and 1958, the scattered leftist organizations merged into a united Egyptian Communist Party and began to re-evaluate their hostility toward the regime, based on its anti-colonial posture. The National Union, which in 1957 replaced the four-year-old Liberation Rally as the sole state-sanctioned political party, approved 1188 candidates for 350 National Assembly seats. It was, many conceded, a step towards political liberalization, although power remained concentrated in the president's office, the army and intelligence service.

The Aswan High Dam was the regime's star project, its symbol of progress toward nationhood and engine for economic development and social betterment, particularly in the countryside. However, before any ground was broken for the dam, a variety of projects, some more successful than others, captured the public attention. Abd al-Latif al-Baghdadi, a Free Officers founding member and Minister of Public Working, undertook to remodel Cairo's fashionable districts. Streets and public squares named for royal personages were renamed to honor liberation, evacuation, the army, the republic and 26 July. A pedestal in the newly designated "Liberation Square," intended to support a statue of Khedive Ismail, remained empty, despite grandiose plans for a revolutionary monument. A state-of-the-art Hilton Hotel was built on the site of the former British barracks; nearby stood the new Shepherd's Hotel, which replaced the landmark building destroyed in the January 1952 riots. Both fronted a broad, Nile-side boulevard, which cut through the lawn of the British embassy. South of Cairo, at Helwan, the Soviets financed a massive steelworks. Outside Alexandria, the 1.2 million feddan Liberation Province was an early model for land reclamation and rural cooperatives (through mixed results, it also became symbolic of bureaucratic inefficiency and the struggle between technocrats and ideologues). Images of hard-working peasants, free from feudal bondage, bringing life to arid soil and tough industrial laborers producing building materials, constructing affordable housing and moving the earth to redirect the waters of the Nile, permeated the national consciousness and filled Egyptians with pride and hope.

The arts blossomed under active state support, though now with revolutionary undercurrents. Egypt had long been the entertainment center of the Arab world, a mecca for musicians, stage and screen stars. The state had controlled the airwaves since the 1930s, but under the Nasser regime the number of stations and the power of their transmitters grew hugely. The film industry, rooted in a studio system that earned it the epithet "Hollywood on the Nile," attracted special attention from a ruling élite enamored of local and international screen idols. From the late forties, Egypt's studios produced fifty to sixty movies a year. The majority were comfortable within the conventions of their genre: musicals, romances, adventures and comedies; but some filmmakers, freed from the constraints imposed by the old regime's censors, began to explore taboo social issues – rural poverty, urban crime, traditional roles, sex and sexuality. A new generation of actors achieved stardom and became associated with the revolutionary project. In 1958, the regime founded the Higher Institute for Cinema to support technical improvements and encourage studio bosses to invest in projects with artistic or literary (rather than pure financial) merit – even to abandon the traditional happy ending. The Ministry of Culture sponsored modern art exhibitions and tours by Western orchestras, dance troupes and jazz bands. Popular magazines featured local starlets on the front cover, while the back covers were reserved for Elizabeth Taylor, Susan Hayward, Audrey Hepburn or Marilyn Monroe.

Egypt's new rulers projected a secular nationalist face for their country. Tharwat Ukasha, a Free Officers insider who (while temporarily banished for leaning too far left) completed a PhD at the Sorbonne, returned to run the ministry of culture, described to me a visit to Bayreuth to hear Wagner's Ring Cycle as his personal *hajj* (pilgrimage). Several founding members of the Free Officers – later RCC members – Husayn al-Shafi'i, Kamal al-Din Husayn and Anwar al-Sadat, reflected a more religious orientation. But none opposed the break with the Muslim Brotherhood, agreeing resolutely with the majority that the Islamist promotion of a faith-based agenda ran counter to the aims of their movement and revolution. The officers brought into their first cabinet, as Minister of Pious Endowments, a reform-minded cleric and former Muslim Brotherhood student leader, Ahmad Hasan al-Baquri. Ahmad Husni, the first Justice

Minister, also had Brotherhood ties. Yet in 1955, the regime outlawed all religious courts and in 1961 nationalized the venerable al-Azhar theological seminary; the Education Ministry oversaw its conversion into a secular university with faculties of arts, sciences, medicine and engineering.

Egypt's Coptic minority, approximately fifteen percent of the national population at the time, particularly strong in Upper Egypt, supported the regime's nationalist and social welfare agenda but increasingly from the sidelines. Egyptian secular nationalism had been founded on the shared symbolism of the crescent and cross, the emblem of the original *Wafd* and the banner of 1919. Coptic politicians, most prominently Makram Ubayd, played leading roles in liberal-era politics, even as the Coptic population witnessed its own internal tensions between lay and religious leaders. Matters briefly came to the boil in 1954 when members of the militant *Movement of the Coptic Nation* abducted the Patriarch, Yusab II, in an effort to force his abdication and convene a synod to elect a successor. In this instance the state intervened, dispatching troops to disperse rebels who had commandeered the patriarchate; a year later the church synod did oust its leader.

The new Patriarch, Kirollos VI, elected in 1959, established cordial relations with Nasser, winning his approval for the building of twenty to thirty new churches per annum and financial support for the construction of a new cathedral. Many lay and religious community leaders complained of discrimination in government representation and civil service promotions, persistent bureaucratic resistance to the approval of building permits and the preponderance of an Islamic orientation (for example the teaching of Arabic) in the educational system. Nasser utilized presidential prerogative to appoint Coptic representatives to parliament but could not shake criticism that he ignored vital Coptic concerns. However, he never faced the outright challenge that his successor, Sadat, did in his later confrontations with Shenouda, who succeeded Kirollos after his death in 1971.

If modern urban Egypt retained its longstanding preferred Western look, it lost much of its cosmopolitan mixed demography. Cairo and Alexandria had been multi-ethnic, poly-religious metropolises, filled with native and foreign-born Greeks, Armenians, Italians and Jews, running the gamut from fabulously wealthy to downtrodden. Many lived in older neighborhoods, like Cairo's Jewish quarter – where the Nasser family resided for a time – that carried religious or ethnically-based names. The rich lived in lavish villas in newer, class-based gated neighborhoods, like Garden City and Zamalek, or suburbs like Maadi and Heliopolis, alongside Egypt's pashas.

In the later years of the liberal era, particularly after World War Two, a trend toward social and cultural "Egyptianization" began to undercut those cosmopolitan foundations. Under a 1929 law, any Ottoman subject resident on 5 November 1914 (the date Britain declared Egypt a protectorate), who had maintained their residency, qualified for Egyptian citizenship (those who arrived afterward had a year in which to apply). In 1950 the law was revised to place a greater burden of proof on applicants to demonstrate residency between 1914 and 1929. A series of measures to insure that Egyptians dominated corporate concerns culminated in 1947 legislation which provided that forty percent of any company board and fifty-one percent of its shares be held by Egyptians. The Palestine conflict provoked anti-Jewish animosity, reflected during the 1948 war in limited but confidence-rattling attacks on Jewish-owned businesses and, in one case, Cairo's Jewish quarter. The palace issued a statement emphasizing the loyalty of the majority of Egypt's Jews but the police arrested several thousand and interned many more in prison camps on the outskirts of Cairo and Alexandria. Rumors of Israeli air strikes, at times supported by government officials, fueled public unease; the authorities later revealed that several blasts had been linked to the Muslim Brotherhood. In the aftermath some twenty thousand Egyptian Jews, approximately one quarter of the population, left the country.

Things later improved, and the military government made overtures to Jewish religious leaders. But in the wake of the "tripartite aggression" the Nasser regime passed legislation to expropriate the wealth of, and to deny, in some cases strip, Egyptian citizenship from "foreign enemies." These laws affected all foreign nationals, particularly British and French subjects, but also Egypt's other foreign minority populations for whom, socially and economically, life became increasingly untenable. There was little, if any, violence comparable to that of 1948 but nearly one thousand Jews were arrested and at least five hundred Jewish-owned firms sequestered. By the end of November 1956, approximately five hundred Jewish heads of household were ordered to leave the country; most took their families with them. A headlong rush of nationalistic, some would say chauvinistic, enthusiasm was captured in a series of propaganda movies featuring fifth-column foreign villains, which intensified the animosity directed at those suddenly deemed non-Egyptian. Jews, Syrians, Greeks, Italians and Armenians left in droves for Europe, Israel and the Americas; usually voluntarily but sometimes under duress and always with tight restrictions imposed on what they could take with them. In the spring of 1957, the government cancelled sequestration orders and relaxed restrictions on personal property leaving the country. By 1958, agreements were concluded with France and Britain that allowed certain people to return, but the momentum could not be halted. The death knells for Egypt's cosmopolitanism were the nationalization decrees. By the outbreak of the June 1967 war, only two and a half thousand Jews remained in Egypt and the Greek population had dwindled, from 140,000 in the early 1950s to approximately 30,000.

For some, even outsiders, the change marked the righting of old wrongs, such as the extra-territoriality enjoyed by foreign subjects and the realization that the cultural "de-Arabicization" of some communities, reflected in their European linguistic and cultural orientation, ran counter to the simultaneous "Egyptianization of state and society" that had been underway well before the Nasser era.[6] Cairo "seems to belong to the people ... the spirit is new and the spirit is powerful," wrote a foreign journalist in 1957. "This is the new Cairo ... a Cairo of which the Cairenes themselves are owners and therefore hosts."[7] Although Egypt never became as mono-cultural as some imagine, years later many would regret the anti-foreign tenor of the post-Suez years and bemoan the precipitate action taken against minorities, many of whom deemed themselves patriots. Ironically, as Egypt became more "Egyptian," outside pressures for it to become more "Arab" increased.

THE ARAB CIRCLE

In his *Philosophy of the Revolution*, Nasser identified three circles of influence in which he saw Egypt as a leader. The Islamic circle never dominated Egyptian policymaking. Nasser went on a pilgrimage to Mecca and pictures of him in the modest dress of a *hajji* were widely circulated. The Islamic congresses to which he sent Anwar al-Sadat and others never appeared to be more than a backdrop. The regime's openly secular self-imaging, the deteriorating relationship with the Saudis and the crack down on the Muslim Brotherhood (linked to the Saudis and, reputedly, covert Western operations against Egypt and Nasser) precluded serious involvement in pan-Islamic politics. Egypt endeavored to play a greater role in African affairs. Nasser was close to Ghana's Kwame Nkrumah (who named one of his sons Gamal) and supported Patrice Lumamba of the Congo. However, the reluctance of many sub-Saharan African leaders to be drawn into the Arab-Israeli conflict – for many, Israel was a model for development; Israeli technical and military

[6] Thomas Philip, *The Syrians in Egypt: 1725–1975* (Stuttgart: Franz Steiner, 1985), p. 144.

[7] Desmond Stewart, cited in Joel Gordon, *Revolutionary melodrama: Popular film and civic identity in Nasser's Egypt* (Chicago: Chicago Studies in the Middle East, 2002), p. 255.

advisors traveled the continent – left Egypt, along with other North African nations, on the margins of the Organization of African Unity.

It was the Arab circle, in which for many Nasser stood as champion, which came to dominate Egypt's attention, although it was not without its share of setbacks.

Arab politics grew increasingly dangerous in the aftermath of Suez. King Saud had been in Egypt during Nasser's show-down with Muhammad Nagib in March 1954 and served as mediator. In 1955, Egypt sent a military mission to Saudi Arabia. Saud, in turn, denounced the Baghdad Pact and during the early part of the Suez War allowed Egyptian planes refuge in his country. By late 1957, however, Saudi-American relations, as well as regular radio broadcasts on Radio Cairo calling for the heads of Arab monarchs, precluded real amity. In March 1956, King Husayn of Jordan dismissed Glubb Pasha, the Brit-ish commander of his Arab Legion, an action which British diplomats (mistakenly) believed to have been orchestrated by Nasser. The election of pro-Nasserist members to the Jordanian parliament in October 1956, on the eve of the Suez War, shook the young king. Husayn arrested his Prime Minster and Chief of Staff, accusing them of plotting a *coup*. Nasser read the move as hostile to Egypt and its local supporters but, recognizing the extent to which the Saudis and Israelis (each for their own reasons) backed the King, confined his retaliation to rhetoric. Iraq's Hashemite monarchy, kin to Jordan's, maintained its pro-British line. There would be no negotiation with Nuri al-Saʻid, the old guard politician who kept Iraq in the Baghdad Pact.

The Americans remained ambivalent. Despite the clearly punitive measure of canceling the high dam loan, the Eisen-hower administration had arguably saved Nasser during the Suez Crisis, first by frustrating Anglo-French diplomatic efforts to marshal support for aggression, then by calling a halt to their invasion. The reservoir of good will quickly dried up and when, in the Eisenhower doctrine, the United States proclaimed its resolve to act against communist infiltrators, Nasser recognized he was a prime target. The CIA drew up various plans to eliminate the Egyptian president, yet never, even in the darkest days of US-Egyptian relations, did the Americans declare outright their enmity or sever ties completely with Nasser. Egypt's leader might be unscrupulous, wily, dangerous and a force to be contained or even rolled back but, ultimately, he was someone with whom one could play what CIA operative Miles Copeland called "the game of nations."

Arab politics reached a crescendo in 1958, as important a year as 1956. In January and February, Egypt and Syria formalized the federated United Arab Republic; in May, the assassination of a prominent anti-government journalist sparked civil war in Lebanon and in July, the Iraqi monarchy fell in a bloody *coup* that resulted in the murder of both King Faysal II and his trusted Prime Minister, Nuri al-Sa`id. Within days of the Iraqi *coup*, the British government dispatched troops to bolster Husayn's grip on the Jordanian throne. Several weeks later, US Marines landed in Lebanon to broker an end to intercommunal conflict. Egypt did not figure directly in any of these upheavals; though Nasser stood symbolically at or near the center of each, his name invoked by all sides in praise or condemnation. However he positioned himself, however he maneuvered to avoid direct action, he could not escape blame for direct support of actions that appeared to undermine his regional enemies. For his supporters, he could rarely, if ever, do enough. In Syria, he could not help but be drawn into the fray.

UNION

The drive for unity with Syria, an idea dangled by pan-Arabist politicians for a number of years, suddenly became urgent in early 1958. Syria's leaders had pressed for closer economic and military integration since 1955. The Suez Crisis put all such talk on hold; early in 1957 Nasser advised Syrian Prime

Minister Sabri al-Asali that the matter required a long-term approach. The Egyptians, he suggested, needed at least five years to take steps. Syrian internal politics kept the issue alive, as unity became an acid test of pan-Arab positioning. A twenty-four member military council, representing "progressive" nationalist forces, worked with civilian politicians – especially the Syrian Ba`th Party– to press the issue in early 1958. Fear of a communist takeover fueled their ardor. The communists also supported union, although many suspected they did so to scare off the Egyptians. The upshot was the military command's abrupt decision to send a delegation to Cairo in mid-January. The mission's leader later described their proposal as if it were, in a sense an ultimatum, driven by popular demand: "The crowds were drunk ... Who at that hour could dare say we do not want unity? The people would tear their heads off.'[8]

Nasser resisted union, an initiative he deemed rooted in negative motivation. Unable to squelch the impetus, he determined to mold it to meet his terms and Egypt's perceived interests. He insisted on formal negotiations with Syrian government representatives, so on 16 January Syria's new Prime Minister, Salah al-Din Bitar, flew to Cairo. He returned to Damascus with Nasser's demands that the Syrian military withdraw from politics, the political parties disband and any federation be approved by popular referendum. Syrian generals and politicians balked at the preconditions but Nasser remained adamant. Bitar returned to Cairo on 26 January, followed five days later by President Shukri al-Quwatli. On 1 February Nasser and Quwatli initialed an agreement; within the week each presented the proposal to their respective legislatures and on 21 February the union was approved by plebiscite. Soon after, Nasser confessed to American embassy officials that it had all been something of a whirlwind. He had undertaken to negotiate personally with the Syrians but had

---

[8] James Jankowski, *Nasser's Egypt, Arab nationalism and the United Arab Republic* (Boulder: Lynne Rienner, 2002), p. 106.

not kept a detailed set of notes and although he had managed to impose his preconditions on a wavering Syrian government, he remained unconvinced it was for the best.

The United Arab Republic, thus, represented a trap for, as much as (if not more than) the culmination of pan-Arab aspirations. At first, the public spectacle evinced tremendous enthusiasm. When Nasser toured Syria shortly after the union, throngs met him at every stop. New anthems dominated the airwaves. Muhammad Abd al-Wahhab's '*al-Watan al-Akbar*' premiered in January 1960 in Aswan, at the foundation stone ceremony for the high dam; a quintessential moment of Egyptian pride and now an Arab affair. After the opening chorus, Abd al-Halim Hafiz sang:

> My nation, my fortune – I love you with all my heart,
> My nation, the nation of the Arabs.
> You, who have been calling for greater unity
> Ever since you beheld the beauty of the revolution.
> You are growing and growing,
> Attaining the glory of days gone by ...

Four female divas, Egyptian, Syrian and Lebanese, then sang. When the gala production was filmed in a studio, for television, an Algerian female vocalist was added. Chorus members dressed as workers, peasants and soldiers carried the new flag, Egypt's revolutionary black, white and red tricolor, with the Egyptian eagle replaced by two green stars.

The equality symbolized by the UAR banner did not truly reflect the reality of a union in which Egypt clearly dominated Syria. The organizational structure of the UAR changed several times during its four-year existence. For a time, the two "provinces" maintained their own currency and regional cabinets exercised separate jurisdiction over finance, justice, agriculture and internal security but Nasser and the Egyptians retained ultimate authority over foreign affairs, defense and education. Nasser was sole president and Cairo the seat of power. Four vice-presidents served under him, two Egyptians and two Syrians, but Egyptians outnumbered Syrians twenty to fourteen in the cabinet. Syrian politicians, with their political organizations dissolved and their parliament remodeled on Egypt's one-party National Union, chafed at restrictions on their politicking. The Communist Party leader, Khalid Bakdash, who had left Syria in February 1958, returned in the autumn to advocate a less rigid federation. Nasser consequently ordered a crackdown on communist activity. By that time, Ba`thist leaders, initially the greatest champions of union, had also grown disillusioned. Syrian officers resented Egyptian domination of the armed forces and intelligence services, as well as inequities in perquisites and salaries. The landed and industrial élite opposed the import, even under more generous terms, of Egypt's agrarian reform and labor legislation, and the middle classes were anxious over plans for a common currency and tighter controls on foreign trade. Egypt could not be blamed for the weather, but in an atmosphere of growing mistrust and resentment, their three-year drought came to symbolize Syria's penance for the rush to unification. The planned imposition of further reforms in the summer of 1961 – the nationalization decrees known as the "July laws" – aggravated relations and left a growing number of Syrians questioning the entire venture.

During his 1961 annual February–March tour of Syria, Nasser felt compelled to discount rumors that Syrian political parties would be reinstated and parliament reopened. He still drew large crowds, but his popularity appeared to have eroded. However, his associates reaped most of the blame. Chief among them was Abd al-Hakim Amr, who, while retaining his command of the combined armed forces, also served as Governor of Syria. Despite a reputation for turning a blind eye to the personal aggrandizement of friends and leading a wild life of romantic affairs and substance abuse, Amr initially was favored by conservative Syrian elements for restraining the implementation of Egypt's agrarian reform in their province. In the end, however, he engaged in a power struggle with the Syrian intelligence chief, Abd al-Hamid al-Sarraj. Initially, it appeared Sarraj had the upper hand; then in August 1961, as part of another restructure, he was appointed vice-president and posted to Cairo. On 26 September Sarraj abruptly resigned and returned to Damascus. Two days later, Syrian army units arrested Amr and the high command. Those who engaged in negotiations with Amr to defuse the crisis said nothing about repealing the union, but when Nasser rejected all talk of reform the rebels put Amr on a plane for Egypt and re-proclaimed Syria's territorial integrity.

Nasser immediately denounced the rebels as reactionar-ies acting at foreign behest. He believed negotiating would convey weakness and presumably suspected that compromise would only postpone the inevitable. Claiming to act on behalf of popular will, he refused formally to disband the UAR and insisted that Egypt would not recognize the new Syrian government but would, however, accept Syria's re-entry into the Arab League. His mistake, he confessed several weeks later, was to try to compromise with "reactionary" forces rather than working to inculcate truly "revolutionary socialist" ideals in Syria. Egypt had already embarked on the road to socialism with the 1961 "July laws" (of which more later) but the Syrian secession was a new phase in Nasserist state building. Arab Socialism of the 1960s cannot be understood outside the context of the failure of the UAR.

JULY 1958 – THREE CRISES

The failed pan-Arab experiment unfolded against a backdrop of regional rivalries and regime instability, which underscored Nasser's earlier reservations about plunging into formal union with Syria. Public sentiment in neighboring Arab states ran strongly in favor of the "greater nation," despite the antagonistic response of their leaders. Lebanon's Maronite President, Camille Chamoun, a vocal proponent of the Eisenhower doctrine, had denounced the UAR from the outset while even less hostile politicians felt compelled to emphasize Lebanese independence. None the less, thousands of Lebanese citizens headed for Damascus to greet Nasser on his first visit there in February 1961. Immediately after declaration of the UAR, Iraq and Jordan announced the formation of a federation, the Union of Arab States, which emphasized the territorial integrity and existing government of its member nations. Iraq's King Faysal took the role of titular head of state and Nuri al-Sa'id became its prime minister. The Saudis who, in January 1958, had briefly engaged in trilateral talks about a more conventional alliance with its Hashemite neighbors, expressed no interest. The Saudis did contact Syrian elements in the hope of financing a military coup and even the assassination of Nasser but Syrian insiders shared this with the Egyptians. Nasser denounced the Saudi king and withdrew Egypt's military mission but rather than break diplomatic relations he worked to promote popular opposition to the royal family. When elements much more favorable to *rapprochement* compelled King Saud to hand greater authority to Crown Prince Faysal, Nasser could chalk up a political victory. With the overthrow of Iraq's monarchy in July 1958, the joint Hashemite initiative collapsed. Nasser and the UAR stood atop the Arab world, despite the intervention of Western military forces to shore up two antagonistic regimes.

The crises of July 1958 developed in rapid succession. On 14 July, the Iraqi military, led by self-styled "Free Officers" working with civilian allies, seized power, killed the King and other members of the royal family and announced the abolition of the monarchy. Nuri al-Sa'id was captured while attempting to flee and brutally murdered a day later. Nasser had been forewarned of an uprising and had expressed his sympathies, while not pressing for details. He was visiting Yugoslavia when news of the uprising broke and quickly extended diplomatic recognition to the rebels. Yet, apprehensive of regional instability, and recalling Suez, he cautioned the Iraqis against provoking the West by moving too quickly, for example by canceling trade

agreements. He stated outright that he felt it was not appropri-
ate at that time to discuss Iraqi entry into the five month-old
UAR. The Ba'thist leader Michel Aflaq hoped Nasser would
visit Baghdad while *en route* to the Soviet Union. Like the
Syrian unionists six months earlier, Aflaq felt that Nasser could
be presented with a *fait accompli* (ironically, it was then that
leading Syrian Ba'thists began to lose faith in the UAR). The
Vice-Premier, Abd al-Salam Arif, also raised the issue of unity
when he visited Cairo shortly afterwards but Nasser told him,
as he now told Aflaq, that too much remained to be worked
out with the Syrians.

The situation grew ever more complex. "It is difficult to
over-estimate the psychological shock caused in London and
Washington and among their remaining Arab allies by the
Iraqi revolution." In one fell swoop the "main pillar of Anglo-
American policy" in the region came crashing down.[9] While
few blamed Nasser directly, many felt he surely stood to gain.
Throughout the spring, Camille Chamoun, whose bid for a
second term had inflamed the situation in Lebanon, denounced
Egyptian interference in his country's affairs and in May, the
Lebanese government charged Egypt with interfering before
both the United Nations and the Arab League. Nasser proposed
US mediation and offered to cut off supplies to Lebanese partisans. Eisenhower's administration, aware that the Lebanese
had overstated Egypt's involvement in the civil war, viewed him
as too much part of the problem to be party to the solution.
After the violent overthrow of their Hashemite allies in Iraq,
the Americans agreed to dispatch troops to Lebanon, even
though by mid-July Chamoun had expressed his willingness
to leave office on completion of his term. US Marines landed
on 14 July; American diplomats helped arrange new elections
and the planned transfer of power to the victor, General Fuad
Shihab. By October all fighting had stopped. Jordan, too,
needed immediate attention. Two days after the Iraqi coup,

[9] Stephens, *Nasser*, p. 287.

King Husayn requested military assistance from the West. Britain dispatched two hundred paratroopers, who remained until the autumn to shore up this surviving Hashemite monarchy. The United States sent fifty million dollars to help counteract Nasserist propaganda and the work of UAR agents on the ground, largely Syrians under the direction of Abd al-Hamid al-Sarraj.

It is indisputable that Nasser, his media services and UAR agents played a hand in backing friendly forces in all three countries. The degree to which he, rather than Sarraj's Syrian agents, directly involved himself is far harder to gauge. Even trickier to answer are questions regarding Nasser's ultimate aims because, while clearly hostile to the Lebanese, the Saudis and the two Hashemite regimes, Nasser recognized that instability beyond his borders could undermine his position and undo his projected development schemes. After Suez, no Western powers ever declared outright war against Egypt but neither did they seek to work too closely with it. Positive neutrality had all but died following his greater reliance on Soviet economic and military assistance. Nasser struggled, even as he took Egypt down the socialist path, to keep all channels open, particularly those to Washington. The irony of the Lebanese solution is that, in one reading, "it was as though the Marines had been brought in to achieve Nasser's objective [the removal of Chamoun and election of Shihab, his compromise candidate] for him." [10]

The troubling direction of the Iraqi revolution, led by men imitating his own Free Officers movement, underlined the dangers of acting too quickly, too soon. In September 1958 Abd al-Salam Arif, the number two man in Baghdad, an ardent pan-Arabist and proponent of close Iraqi-Egyptian ties, was shunted off to West Germany as ambassador. Power now rested more firmly in the hands of Abd al-Karim Qasim, Prime Minister and

---

[10] Miles Copeland, *The game of nations* (New York: Simon & Schuster, 1969), p. 272.

commander of the army, who adopted an increasingly nationalist posture pitting Baghdad against Cairo (and Damascus) in
ways that recalled the long-term rivalry with Nuri al-Sa'id.
Qasim also looked increasingly to communist allies at home
and abroad for support. In March 1959, pro-Nasser units,
in league with Syrian agents, staged an abortive rebellion in
Mosul, which was suppressed at the cost of hundreds of casualties. Nasser decried Qasim as an agent of imperialism and,
playing on his name, the "divider" of unity in the region.

The second year of the UAR, following the tumultuous
events of 1958, saw a general cooling of regional tensions. By
the summer of 1959, Nasser and Qasim had reopened channels of communication and Saudi Arabia's Faysal and Lebanon's
Fuad Shihab appeared more willing than their predecessors to
treat with Nasser. Egypt's relationship with Jordan proved the
most rocky. In August 1960, the Prime Minister was killed
by a bomb planted in his office. Palestinian Jordanians were
implicated but fingers were also pointed at Jordanian exiles
in Syria, along with Syrian security agents. Renewed insults
ensued, yet in early 1961 Husayn and Nasser began to discuss
a *rapprochement*. The communications produced nothing and
the discussions collapsed during the crisis surrounding Syrian
secession from the UAR but the period of calm emphasized
the political uncertainties of the early 1960s.

Nasser's prestige, according to foreign observers and even
regional supporters, had plummeted: the effects of the honey-
moon of Bandung and Suez had worn off. The "greater nation"
project, undertaken with reservations, even cynicism, had
ground to a halt. Nasser recognized the trap in which he had
allowed himself to become ensnared. As an Arab leader, he
would be called upon, often cynically, to promote pan-Arab
unity, to defend neighboring states from imperialism or Israeli
aggression and to speak on behalf of Palestinian national aspirations. He might have recognized the trap but could never quite
escape the burden of leader of the Arab world. This was to have
resounding implications in the second decade of his rule.

The first decade had taken its toll. Nasser had not yet developed the serious ailments that would kill him at fifty-two but already in the early 1960s, despite the touched-up, matinee-idol official portraits, he looked older than his age. He had put on weight and walked less erectly. There was also a personal toll. Syria's secession from the UAR nearly destroyed his relationship with Abd al-Hakim Amr, the second most powerful man in the country. For a brief period the two did not speak to each other; only through the exertions of old friends was a showdown averted. It remains unclear whether Nasser or others understood the extent to which the Field Marshal failed to address the inadequacies of Egypt's armed forces, which should have been recognized during the Suez War.

As Egypt faced a new decade, there was much about which to be optimistic. The High Dam was nearing completion. Television, halted by Suez, was preparing to begin transmission. Cinemas, schools and clinics went up throughout the countryside. The army, to judge from holiday parades, was impressively well-furnished with Soviet equipment. The universities boomed. Women were working their way up the ladder in the bureaucratic, academic and corporate worlds. Many would later argue that this was all a grand illusion but, for the time being, it was a captivating one.

3

THE SOCIALIST GARDEN:
1961–1967

Overlooking the socialist garden, we stand checking on the
    waters,
A nation of heroes, scientists and workers,
And with us, Gamal, singing a joyous song.
All of us calling the peasant call,
To his brothers at the hour of irrigation ...
[*Bustan al-ishtirakiya* (The Socialist Garden), 1964]

The anthems and popular iconography of early and mid-
1960s Egypt almost invariably refer to discrete manifesta-
tions of the socialist projects undertaken before the breakup of
the UAR, which were intensified in response to Syrian secession. For the tenth anniversary of the July Revolution, the most
powerful and beloved lyricists evoked pride in accomplishment
and demanded sustained progress. The high dam was central to
the nation's imagination, ornamented by images of determined
peasants, workers, soldiers and engineers; male and female.
The *tarbush,* once proudly worn by the intelligentsia and the
educated middle class, now appeared only in comic guise or
historical drama as an outmoded anachronism. Students and
professional workers, men and women, were bareheaded. As
the decade progressed, men's hair grew lusher and women's
more closely cropped, pants got tighter and skirts shorter. For
the urban middle and upper classes, at least, tradition seemed
to hang in the balance.

This cultural revolution meshed with the broader social revolution undertaken by the Nasser regime. Nasser's response to the breakup of the UAR, in large part due to the nationalization decrees of the late fifties and early sixties, was to push faster. The Charter of National Action (commonly known as the National Charter), announced in 1962, came on the heels of bitter denunciations of feudal reactionaries and self-criticism of the regime's failure to break with the classes and forces that worked to undermine progress and social justice. The Charter created a vast public sector to administer key components of the economy, as well as another phase of political reorganization. The after-effects still spark partisan and non-partisan reflection and re-evaluation. Undoubtedly, in many respects, the regime grew more authoritarian – but were the means to good or bad ends?

Arab dreams were not abandoned with Syria's secession but they were tempered. Once the initial shock and anger abated, Nasser realized where the project had gone wrong. Regional politics grew more confusing. Egypt remained center stage and

Socialist Garden. Work on the high dam at Aswan, the symbol of the revolutionary state, from a period postcard. (Property of the author.)

Nasser was still the impresario but he found himself compelled to take increasing risks to retain his dominant role. In the Yemen, Egypt became embroiled in a military quagmire that debilitated the economy, sapped morale and highlighted tensions within the officer *corps*, the nation's new power élite.

The Arab-Palestinian-Israeli conflict masked inter-Arab tensions. A close examination of the run up to the June 1967 war reinforces the conclusion that, amidst a plethora of mis-steps and miscues, Nasser had been drawn into a showdown that he had hoped to avoid, largely because of his self-styled leadership of the Arab world. In the aftermath, his revolutionary project ground to a halt. The shining anthems to the socialist garden were mothballed and virtually forgotten.

ARAB SOCIALISM

The National Charter has antecedents in the widespread nationalizations decreed in July 1961, the Revolution's ninth anniversary. The impulse behind them, however, may be traced to the regime's earliest days, the first decade of Nasser's rule. In their *Six Principles*, the Free Officers spoke of freeing Egypt from feudalism and the "domination of capital and monopoly over government." In October 1952, the regime established a National Production Council charged with drafting a three-year development program. Throughout the 1950s, the government sought to further the Egyptianization of industry that had begun in the years before the Free Officers takeover. After the Suez War, all British and French-owned companies and properties were sequestered. Article 1 of the Constitution of the National Union described Egypt as "a socialist, democratic, co-operative society, free of all social and political exploitation." Yet until the late 1950s, the regime placed faith in what it called "guided capitalism," trusting Egypt's national capitalists to work in tandem with the state to promote economic growth with a human face.

Between January 1957 and July 1961 growing concerns about the pace of economic development and the perceived unwillingness of private enterprise to collaborate with the state led to a series of dramatic structural reforms. In its first major moves, the regime replaced the National Production Council with a National Planning Commission and founded a semi-autonomous Economic Organization to control industries that were fully or partially government owned, as well as sequestered foreign firms. The government also ordered the remaining foreign banks, insurance companies and commercial import-export firms to become Egyptian-owned within five years. In 1958, the Ministry of Industry announced a five-year development plan to increase the growth rate of industrial output from six to sixteen percent. In 1960, the regime nationalized Bank Misr, the powerful financial industrial and commercial conglomerate, founded in 1920, which accounted for some twenty percent of industrial production and instituted the first comprehensive five-year plan.

Dispirited by the powerful autonomy of Egyptian capitalists, eager to institute a more state-centred economic regime and increasingly concerned with the degree to which Syrian private interests resisted such trends, Nasser and his associates resolved to assert even greater authority at home. The July laws, which were effectively a second, social revolution, nationalized major sectors of the economy. Banks, insurance companies, real estate corporations and heavy industry fell under state control. The state expropriated half the capital of eighty-six mid-sized companies and limited personal holdings in over one hundred others. Only light industry and "non-exploiting" professions remained fully in private hands. In agriculture, the regime instituted a revised land reform, limiting family holdings to one hundred feddans (the original limit had been two hundred).

Introspective, but with a flair for capturing the political moment, Nasser responded to the immediate challenge of

Syrian secession "with characteristic vigour and defiance." [1]
He reshuffled his government, appointing five former Free
Officer comrades as vice presidents. Egypt would retain its
role as leader of the "Arab revolution" but would not entertain
thoughts of formal unity with any nation that had not yet liberated itself. In a televised address in October 1961, he admitted
that he had placed too much faith in the patriotism of "reactionary" forces. To insure greater representation of workers and
peasants the National Union needed to be restructured.

The regime also enacted further punitive measures against
leading capitalists. In October 1961, the government sequestered 157 "reactionary capitalists" and ordered forty prominent
figures to be arrested. The number of sequestrations climbed
to six hundred the following month. Virtually all of those
arrested were released by mid-February the next year and several sequestration orders were rescinded, but twelve thousand
people lost their political rights. The regime made examples
of the most prominent capitalists, such as Ahmad Abbud, who
was reportedly worth thirty million Egyptian pounds. Calls for
a more open political process, even from friends and former
comrades, fell upon deaf ears.

On 21 May 1962, in a five-hour speech to the National
Congress of Popular Forces, Nasser introduced the Charter of
National Action. The President drew clear distinctions between
Arab socialism and Marxism. Egypt's path would curtail free
enterprise in key sectors, and the state would play a direct role
in economic development, but capitalism would not be totally
abolished. Likewise, the Arab revolution would not be rooted
in class struggle. The enemies remained "imperialism and its
agents" and "unenlightened religious fanaticism." Egypt's communists were chastised for following a foreign lead, although
the specter of the Muslim Brotherhood remained the chief
domestic concern. Nasser drew the boundaries of the new

---

[1] Stephens, *Nasser*, p. 344.

public sector: finance, heavy and medium industry, mining, foreign trade and at least half of domestic trade would be nationalized. Heavy industry would become a state priority; in light industry the public sector would play only a guiding role. On 30 June, after nearly a month of debate, the National Congress assented to the Charter. Two days later, Nasser revealed his intention to restructure the National Union into a new Arab Socialist Union (the ASU). Structurally, there would be little difference, but new rules prescribed that half the representatives would come from the agricultural and industrial working class.

The "July laws" and the National Charter ushered in a new phase of the Nasserist experiment. In 1963, the public sector comprised the largest contributor to GDP. By the end of 1964, most of Egypt's large companies, around eight hundred organizations, had been nationalized. Banking, insurance, investment companies, publishing and the media were taken into the public sector. The government budgeted for sixty percent of the GNP and directed one quarter of national investment toward industrial production.

By 1965, 1.25 million feddans had become available for redistribution. Even this amount, plus the 840,000 feddans already distributed, affected only ten percent of the rural population. A series of measures were enacted to tighten regulations on rent, tenancy and sharecropping and to enforce a minimum agricultural wage, promising greater equity. A further 500,000 feddans lay on reclaimed land. State planning underlay the transformations. Egypt, Nasser proclaimed, aimed to produce everything "from the seed to the missile."

Was this socialism? The iconography meshed national symbols – peasants, workers, Nubians and unveiled women – with the muscles of socialist realism. Anthems of the period speak openly of a socialist revolution in which all Egyptians would take part. On Revolution Day, 1962, Abd al-Halim Hafiz sang:

The Revolution's path is the path to victory.
Long live the army, long live Egypt!
From the day of our revolution's triumph,
With our army, the guardian of our Arab identity,
Each day a new victory arises ...
[*Mutalib al-sha`b* (The People's Demands), 1962]

A year later, his song was of socialist responsibility:

This is responsibility held dear, the love of spirit and freedom.
The affection of a soldier for his weapon – and more.
But what am I by myself?
There is no 'me' – there is 'we', my comrades.
Me and you and he and she – it is our duty to build socialism.
[*Al-Mas'uliya* (Responsibility), 1963]

In 1964, he sang of Egypt as a "socialist garden" and asked
Nasser to transform the country, just as the high dam would:

Good begets good – this joy was yearned for.
The Arab people have thrown off their chains, stepped out of
their yokes.
They are rising to the summit, where they will plant the banner.

Many of the images of the sixties are linked to technology, science, industry and public health. A government publication celebrating the Revolution's fourteenth anniversary proclaimed: "Our country has become a symbol of struggle for freedom and for the construction of a new socialist society, based on sufficiency, justice and hard fruitful work."

Debate has raged ever since. The eminent economic historian, Charles Issawi, described Egypt in 1962 as a "totalitarian socialist state." [2] Leftist critics insisted this was a bourgeois revolution, led by middle class sons and that the persistence of authoritarian rule, even if camouflaged by mass politi-

[2] Charles Issawi, *Egypt in revolution: An economic analysis* (London: Oxford University Press, 1963), p. 47.

cal organizations, could never account for the desires of the masses. Anouar Abdel-Malek, an Egyptian Marxist widely read outside the Arab world, stated bluntly that "planning and statism are absolutely not synonymous with socialism."[3] Forty years on from the Revolution, an Egyptian economist, Riad El Ghonemy, admits difficulty in discerning precisely "what was meant by" socialism.[4] The results were undoubtedly mixed: for various reasons, some beyond Egypt's control, economic development never reached the levels anticipated in the two five-year plans of the 1960s.

Import substitution was promoted as an economic strategy to develop a local industrial base. However, foreign exchange problems and the priority given to expensive, relatively unproductive heavy industries – such as iron, steel and automobile production – kept industrial output well below target. Some industries and technology out-paced consumer demand or even the capability for consumers to use certain products. Bureaucratic inertia, a chronic ailment, proliferated. In the countryside, rapid population growth strained an already unmanageable person-to-land ratio, negating achievements in land reclamation and land reform. Despite efforts to close loopholes and reduce the amount of land allowed per family, large clans managed their holdings in ways that allowed them to retain economic and social power. Overall, the decade was marked by mounting discontent at the rising cost of living and a growing antipathy toward the emergent military élite which enjoyed benefits – salary, housing, professional connections – denied to others.

[3] Anouar Abdel-Malek, *Egypt: Military society* (New York: Vintage, 1968), p. 368.
[4] M. Riad al-Ghonemy, 'An assessment of Egypt's development strategy, 1952–1970' in Elie Podeh and Onn Winckler, *Rethinking Nasserism: Revolution and historical memory in modern Egypt* (Gainesville: Florida University Press, 2004), p. 256.

Whatever the success and failures in both the industrial and agricultural sectors, and however great the disappointments, Egypt was indeed undergoing revolutionary transformation. What had been, on the eve of the Free Officers *coup*, an overwhelmingly agrarian nation, had witnessed the growth of industry to greater than twenty percent GNP. Foreign ownership of capital had been almost eliminated and inequalities of wealth and income substantially narrowed. More people worked in factories and under better conditions, while peasants and small farmers had increased access to co-operatives, interest-free loans, agricultural experts and veterinarians. Public health, particularly in rural areas, showed a marked improvement. Infant mortality had dropped and life expectancy increased. One new school was built every day. Compulsory education for children aged six to twelve, mandated prior to the Revolution but after it enforced with greater diligence, had more than doubled the number of primary school students between 1952 and 1966. Just under half of the students were girls, which meant three-quarters of eligible children attended primary school. Preparatory and secondary school enrolments also hugely increased. After 1957, Egypt boasted four major universities, not including al-Azhar, the thousand-year-old theological seminary which was nationalized into a fully-fledged, state-run university. Female graduates began to enter the white-collar work force in greater numbers. In 1961, just under one percent of the female labor force held executive or management positions, but the number began to climb steadily. Popular culture, films particularly, highlighted women's aspirations and the resultant social tensions, often in comedy. In *Lil rijal faqat* (For Men Only), released in 1964, two sexy female petroleum engineers pose as men in order to escape office confinement and gain access to the oil fields. Two years later, *Mrati mudir amm* (My Wife is General Director) spoofed the battle of the sexes, when a man found himself working under his wife's supervision in a government office.

CULTURAL REVOLUTIONS

Nowhere were the transformations more marked than in the arts and broadcast media. State control of radio pre-dated the Revolution; but the number of national stations and broadcast hours increased under Nasser. *Sawt al-Arab* began in 1953, broadcasting locally for half an hour a day, but quickly expanded to reach regional Arab audiences for nearly eight hours a day. A precursor to transnational satellite television, the station sent correspondents into the field to cover national liberation struggles and transmitted multi-lingual broadcasts throughout the Third World. Television broadcasts, postponed in the wake of the Suez War, began in 1961 with coverage of the opening of the National Assembly. By the latter part of the decade, three channels broadcast for some twenty hours per day. Although it would take years for television to supplant radio as the primary broadcast media (radio is still celebrated in Egypt, even if its influence has waned), those early years, with broadcasts of popular stage plays, early dramatic serials, cinema re-runs, variety shows and holiday specials, are regarded as a golden age; many of the early newsreaders and variety hosts, like their 1950s radio counterparts, are revered as pioneers.

The film industry was not nationalized outright in the 1960s; the public sector co-existed with privately-owned studios. As with the entire socialist venture, cultural state control produced mixed results, both at the box office and in product quality. Public sector production matched, and at times surpassed, private sector, although in the 1960s there was a marked decrease in the number of films produced. Many public sector films, including some that flopped commercially, were later recognized as classics. Bureaucratic rigidity and the politicization of the industry arguably constrained creativity at times. However, two generations of Egypt's best film-makers, many still active, trained under the auspices of the state film institute and got their break in state-funded projects. Some drifted to the commercial sector, while others pushed the industry in new directions, particularly after the 1967 June War, when state censors tolerated more open, pointed criticism of Nasserist shortcomings, particularly authoritarian structures.

DEMOCRACY?

The Nasserist search for a new political order to mobilize national unity and allow for the free expression of popular will proved elusive. His unwillingness to democratize was arguably Nasser's weak point. In March 1965, he swept to a 99.99% electoral victory. Some close associates suggested he might have even greater power were he to win a truly competitive race. Calls for a more open political system persisted, as did the debate concerning the proper progressive role of the growing intelligentsia. The failure of many intellectuals to rally to the new order was termed the "crisis of the intelligentsia." Many expressed a growing concern at the preponderance of "people of trust" in high office at the expense of "people of expertise."

Aside from greater enforced representation by workers and peasants, the Arab Socialist Union differed little from earlier experiments to create a unified single party. Like the National Union, it was organized from the bottom up via village, district and provincial councils. However, a secret, insular, vanguard organization insured the real concentration of power was at the top. Even as Egyptians flocked to join the ASU, often to advance and protect personal, rather than national, interests, the vanguard advanced the powerful cliques which Egyptians would come to refer to with scorn as the "centers of power."

Despite its persistent criticism of Arab socialism as neither true socialism nor representative of popular will, the Egyptian left struck a tactical bargain with the state that allowed an uneasy symbiotic relationship to emerge in the 1960s. In 1957–58, with many of its members in prison, a disparate group of competing, at times ideologically antagonistic Marxist organizations merged into a united Egyptian Communist Party. The Egyptian left approved of Nasser's commitment to national liberation movements, warily supported early nationalization decrees and at times benefited from Egypt's links to the Soviet Union. Nasser's antagonistic relationship with communists in Syria and Iraq rankled but the National Charter persuaded Egypt's communists to reconsider their hostile orientation. In 1965, after extensive negotiations with regime representatives, the ECP voluntarily dissolved; party members joined the ASU and many moved into the higher ranks of the vanguard organization. Marxist economy and historiography flourished on university campuses and leading culture critics published influential journals such *al-Tali`a* (The Vanguard). Communist ideologues were kept under close surveillance and quickly learned their limitations. Class struggle remained off-limits but socialist ideology merged with the progressive, modernist orientation of Nasserism to produce a lively, forward looking, secular generation.

The Muslim Brotherhood remained the great alternative to Nasser's secular thrust, even though it ostensibly had been crushed as an active organization in the early years of Free Officer rule. Many thousands of its members were arrested after the unsuccessful attempt on Nasser's life in October 1954. Those not brought to trial were released in the mid-1950s; many joined the scores of Brothers who had fled the country. Significant numbers sought refuge in the Gulf, where, albeit under the watchful eyes of conservative monarchical regimes, they continued to publish political and religious texts and begin to reconstitute the movement. The Brotherhood remained the great bogey of domestic terror, their acts of violence recalled, for example, in the 1961 debates on democracy after the breakup of the UAR. None the less, in 1964, at the personal urging of Iraqi President Abd al-Salam Arif and ostensibly for health reasons, the regime released Sayyid Qutb, the movement's leading ideologue. Qutb had collaborated with the

Free Officers during a brief period of amity in 1953 but had later been arrested, imprisoned and tortured.

Qutb's half-year of freedom (he was re-arrested in August 1965 together with some four hundred Brothers and charged with treason) is cloaked in mystery. He had kept active while behind bars; his thirty-volume commentary on the Qur'an secured his reputation as one of the most influential Islamic modernist thinkers of the twentieth century. Another, shorter text, a stirring call for vanguard action against the modern apostate state, had been circulating in militant circles for several years. *Ma`alim fi al-tariq* (Milestones along the Path) took Qutb, and a new generation of Muslim Brothers, into direct confrontation with the Nasser regime. Whether Qutb himself actively conspired to overthrow the political order (as he was charged) or whether such a plot even existed cannot be verified. In August 1966, after a show trial accompanied by a virulent media campaign, Qutb went to the gallows, a new Islamist martyr. More moderate Brothers, including Hasan al-Hudaybi, the movement's Supreme Guide, denounced his tract as deviant. For growing numbers of young Islamists, of whom many had, like Qutb, suffered horribly at the hands of state police, and for others who had lost faith in a gradualist approach focused on preaching and education, Qutb's ardent tone resonated deeply.

The specter of the old regime, which had by the mid-60s begun to fade appreciably, occasionally re-emerged. The Nasserist vanguards feared a renewed nostalgia for the liberal era. The most significant moment was in August 1965, when Mustafa al-Nahhas, the venerable leader of the *Wafd*, died at eighty-six years old. Fifteen years earlier, as leader of the last elected government of the liberal era, his inability to tackle political corruption had disappointed Egyptians, who lost faith in the parliamentary order. Despite this, thousands turned out for his funeral, defying bans on demonstrations and the government's refusal to allow Nahhas to be buried alongside his compatriot, Sa`d Zaghlul, in the latter's massive, almost pharaonic, mausoleum near the parliament buildings in Cairo. The approaching fiftieth anniversary of the 1919 revolution re-opened academic debate on its successes and shortcomings, the parliamentary order it engendered and the historical logic of the Free Officers' inheritance of the national movement.

Public stirrings of discontent remained few. At times, the regime displayed little tolerance, even for light-hearted satire. A popular comic who spoofed the nationalizations in a stand-up routine in 1962 was imprisoned for a few nights. Such seeming intolerance hinted at more serious trouble behind the scenes, especially within the ruling élite. Following the proclamation of the National Charter, Nasser brought several of his oldest colleagues together to form a presidential council. However, old amities had eroded.

The discord centered on Abd al-Hakim Amr, Nasser's close friend, who in 1953 became commander-in-chief of the armed forces and was appointed Minister of War a year later. Despite losing his nerve during the Suez War, when he advocated retreat and the resignation of the revolutionary command, compelling Nasser to assume direct control of battlefield strategy, Amr retained his power, attaining, in 1958, the unprecedented rank of field marshal. He was popular in Syrian circles – the kind face of unity – and was not ill-treated by the rebels who detained him in Damascus on the eve of secession. He, however, felt personally humiliated. Fearful that he might become the scapegoat at home, Amr drew a clique of supporters, powerful allies based in the military and state security, more closely around him. His public and private gallivanting with starlets, and well-founded rumors of drug and alcohol abuse, continued unabated, starting rumors of a parallel power structure that might spark a showdown within the leadership.

Backed by key comrades, Nasser determined to clip Amr's wings. Amr agreed to yield operational command of the military to a professional soldier (who would change every three to four years) and accepted the title of Vice-President for Military Affairs. However, he rejected calls by his fellow vice-presidents for him to cede, to the presidential council, control of high-level appointments and promotions. In March 1962, Amr stormed out of a heated council meeting and announced his resignation. Nasser toyed with accepting it, but when word arrived that the Field Marshal had left for the Western Desert and that several of his commanders had also tendered their resignations, the President baulked at an irremediable break. Members of the old guard brought Amr back to the table, where Nasser pacified him by reinstating him as supreme commander. Amr, for his part, bowed to demands for the resignations of commanders who had allied with him. In April 1964, when Nasser disbanded the presidential council and re-ordered his executive, he appointed Amr the first of seven vice-presidents. The 1962 truce proved to be the beginning of the real split between the two old comrades but, none the less, they retained a deep affection. The Field Marshal realized the extent to which the military preserved his power base, the President the degree to which the "spoiled child" – his own designation for Amr – had "grown fangs and claws." [5] Amr's closest, and potentially most dangerous compatriots, Shams Badran, director of Amr's office (soon to be Minister of War) and Salah Nasr, chief of General Intelligence, were allowed to retain their positions, largely because Nasser hoped to use them to keep the Field Marshal in check.

HOT AND COLD WARS

The Nasserist project faced its greatest, and ultimately gravest setbacks, abroad. Nasser clung stubbornly to the facade of the United Arab Republic (not until 1971 did Anwar al-Sadat dispense with the title and proclaim the Arab Republic of Egypt) but secession strengthened his resolve to avoid such formal

[5] Ahmad Hamrush, *Qissat thawrat 23 Yulyu: Abd al-Nasir wa al-Arab* (Cairo: Madbuli, 1976), p. 214.

entanglements in the future. Nasser could not, however, turn his back on regional politics, nor could he ignore verbal challenges from his neighbors to live up to his billing as the champion of Arab unity and liberation. Instability within the ruling elements of republican Syria and Iraq and the coy maneuverings of royal rivals in Hashemite Jordan and Saudi Arabia, compounded by East-West global competition and local problems associated with resurgent Palestinian nationalism and Israel's failure to carve out a secure niche for the Zionist state in the Middle East, frustrated Nasser's revolutionary goals.

Diplomatically, until the lid blew off in June 1967, the sixties were best characterized (as by Malcolm Kerr) as the era of the "Arab Cold War." So long as it remained a war of words, however heated, Nasser could bend regional leaders to his will. Then, in February 1963, Ba'thist rebels in Iraq deposed and murdered Nasser's erstwhile revolutionary rival, Abd al-Karim Qasim and placed the friendly Abd al-Salam Arif in power. A month later the Ba'th Party seized power in Syria. Reluctantly bowing to public pressure, the new Iraqi and Syrian leaders promoted a fresh round of unity talks, including Algeria and Yemen. Nasser hosted the most important gathering in Cairo in April. On his home turf, the undisputed leader of the Arabs dominated the talks by his intellectual ability, tactical skill and sheer force of personality. He "artfully" switched moods, sometimes listening and arguing patiently with an apparent "readiness to compromise," then suddenly moving into "a ruthless, sometimes vindictive attack or a penetrating and often humorous analysis of opposing themes and personalities."[6]

The talks concluded with a standard commitment to a federal agreement that the Egyptians barely took seriously. Shortly after, Nasser left on a month-long tour of Algeria and Yugoslavia, then attended the founding meeting of the Organization of African Unity in Ethiopia. While he was away, the Egyptian press reported that he would no longer co-operate with the

---

[6] Stephens, *Nasser*, pp. 403–4.

Syrians. Later that summer, in July 1963, the Syrian Ba'th Party purged pro-Egyptian members; an attempted *coup* was foiled and twenty-seven rebels executed.

A cooling-off period between the putative allies followed, primarily due to heightened tensions on hotter fronts. In 1964, Nasser found himself caught up in a debilitating civil war in the Yemen, to which he had already committed forty thousand troops. The Yemen Civil War had been sparked by a *coup d'état* which overthrew the antiquated Zaydi dynasty in late September 1962. Like the self-styled Free Officers who had overthrown the Hashemite monarchy in Iraq, the Yemeni rebels, many of whom had undergone military training in Egypt, were inspired by Nasser's July Revolution. Despite rumors of his death, Imam Muhammad (who had succeeded his father, Imam Ahmad, only eight days before), re-surfaced in the northern mountains. From there, with the support of local tribal leaders and Saudi financial and military assistance, he mounted a royalist offensive. Faced with Saudi intervention and the radical republican orientation of the rebels, Nasser felt compelled to offer support to Abd Allah Sallal's new regime. His military command assured him that, with moderate aid, the republicans would crush the resistance and so he committed advisors, technicians, air force units and, ultimately, ground troops to the republican cause. He later admitted that Egypt's military intervention had been a "miscalculation." [7] To most observers, the period became known as "Egypt's Vietnam."

Egyptian troops quickly became bogged down in a conflict that could never be resolved by force. By late 1962, the republican forces were confined to the coast, unable to cut off rebel supply lines in the high interior. Increasingly desperate to turn the corner militarily, Egyptian planes dropped napalm and sent raids across the border into Saudi Arabia. The United States, which recognized the Sallal government in December 1962, attempted to broker a diplomatic solution.

[7] Stephens, *Nasser*, p. 391

Egyptian and Saudi representatives met on numerous occasions and, in June 1963, agreed to a United Nations observer mission. The best that could be said for these efforts was that they forestalled the potential for greater escalation. By 1965, with some seventy thousand troops deployed, Nasser kept his forces on the ground more to affect British policy in Aden than to achieve victory in the Yemen. He had lost patience with Sallal, who now fronted a dissident republican faction which wanted Egypt out. The Saudis, too, began to lose interest in the conflict and complain of their protégés' maverick attitudes. Despite commitments by both Egypt and Saudi Arabia to the achievement of a negotiated settlement, scattered fighting dragged on into 1967. Only in after the June Arab-Israeli war did Nasser and the Saudi King, Faysal, agree to withdraw forces. President Sallal denounced the accord, but by November 1967, he had fled Yemen.

The Yemen intervention remains largely unspoken about in the official historical memory of Nasser's Egypt. Casualty counts vary widely. The war sapped the energies of the armed forces, a key factor when assessing Egypt's performance in the June War. Whether it sapped the morale of the officer *corps* remains unclear; some officers, far from the front, did profit from enhanced salaries and promotions. The adventure took its toll on the deteriorating relationship between Nasser and Abd al-Hakim Amr. Key miscalculations could be laid at Amr's feet. At the same time, however costly in terms of resources and manpower, some have argued that Nasser placed Egypt on the "right side of history" in supporting Yemen's emancipation from an antiquated, repressive regime.[8]

TOWARD RUIN

In the years leading up to June 1967 Nasser's Egypt had pride of

[8] Stephens, *Nasser*, p. 431.

place in the pantheon of newly liberated states. If Nasser found himself assailed alternately by "progressive" and "reactionary" Arab leaders, he retained the (at times grudging) favor of the Soviet Union. When Nikita Khruschev inaugurated the High Dam in May 1964, he bantered with Nasser about the respective merits of Communism and Arab socialism, then handed over one hundred million Egyptian pounds for industrial projects. "The Arab people of Egypt have now passed through the stage of the great socialist transformation," proclaimed the yearbook published by the Ministry of Information. "Imbued with the same strong will and with the same stout resolution, they have embarked upon the stage of the great 'take-off' in order to press forward towards the realization of a better life."

There were always darker sides. In May 1966, in the rural Delta village of Kamshish, an ASU labor organizer was murdered. Salah Maqlad became a socialist martyr, and fingers pointed towards members of a landed family. Within days of the incident, the government charged a Higher Committee for the Liquidation of Feudalism with investigating the degree to which land reform had succeeded or failed to transform rural society.

The committee, headed by Abd al-Hakim Amr and his allies, engaged in a "massive witch hunt against traditional influence in hundreds of villages." In several months of hearings, the committee uncovered evidence regarding the degree to which the rural élite circumvented agrarian reforms by apportioning land among wide kinship networks, confirming critics' charges that "the revolutionary claims of the ruling class were unsupported by conditions in the countryside." [9] Yet, far more than anything else, the committee served to underline the regime's authoritarian face and most of its decrees were rescinded after the June 1967 war. For Amr, his work on the committee meant

[9] Hamied Ansari, *Egypt: The stalled society* (Albany: SUNY Press, 1986), p. 20.

further preoccupation with matters unrelated to his primary charge, Egypt's armed forces.

The road to June 1967 is marked by a series of gambles, most undertaken by Nasser in the context of heightened tensions on the borders between Israel and its Arab neighbors, and by escalating rhetoric that no one appeared ready or able to stifle. The unresolved status both of Israel's place in the Arab Middle East and of the Palestinian diaspora was a major source of regional disquiet, although it was never at the center of Nasser's political consciousness. In the aftermath of the Suez War, Egypt accepted the deployment of a 3400-man United Nations Emergency Force (UNEF) at strategic points along the Egyptian-Israeli border, in the Gaza Strip and on the Sinai coast, and especially in areas close to the Tiran Straits, through which Israel-bound shipping moved towards the Red Sea port of Eilat. The Israeli-Egyptian front stayed relatively quiet during the following decade, even as hostilities erupted with growing frequency along Israel's eastern borders with Syria and Jordan. However, following the proclamation of the UAR, Syria's border effectively became Egypt's. Nasser found himself directly involved in crisis management which did not end with the breakup of official Egyptian-Syrian unity.

Water and waterways were points of contention that on several occasions threatened to spark military conflict. Egypt avoided a diplomatic crisis in 1959, when a Danish freighter bound for Israel attempted to pass through the Suez Canal; ship and crew were released but the cargo was impounded. In 1963, the Israeli government announced unilateral plans to divert the waters of the Jordan River, which it shared with its neighbors, into its own national irrigation system. Nasser forestalled Syrian calls for armed aggression, urging the Arabs instead to use as much water as possible before the Jordan reached Israel.

It was guerilla activity directed against Israel, generally followed by disproportionately forceful counter-raids, which really threatened to upset the delicate situation. Violent encounters persisted throughout the early 1960s, in an environment of escalating rhetoric of Palestinian self-determination. The refugee population had grown from the three-quarters of a million who had been expelled or fled their homes in 1948, to well over one million, two-thirds of whom were judged by the UN to be impoverished. Egypt loudly supported the Palestinian cause, inaugurating the Voice of Palestine radio station and backing the appointment of a Palestinian delegate to the Arab League political committee in September 1963. Concurrently, Nasser alleged that his Arab neighbors sought to push Egypt into unilateral war. In 1964 Egypt backed the formation of the Palestine Liberation Organization and its adjunct the Palestine Liberation Army, both with headquarters in Gaza. Nasser viewed the PLO, led by Ahmad al-Shuqayri, as a potential brake on autonomous Palestinian activism. By the mid-1960s, however, he found himself caught in the crossfire between a vocal minority, led by Tunisia's Habib Bourguiba, who advocated settled relations with Israel and a growing call, always loudest from Syria, for Egypt to expel the UNEF, shut the Tiran Straits to Israeli shipping and begin the liberation of Palestine. Nasser attempted to shout down both sides, reinforcing Egypt's resistance to following any others' lead, yet reminding his hawkish detractors that, with over fifty thousand troops engaged in the Yemen, war was not a viable option.

Looking beyond his regional detractors, Nasser sought to repair a recent rift with the United States. Relations had remained cordial with the Kennedy administration. The Americans funneled economic aid through the Food for Peace program, recognized the Yemeni republic and endeavored to foster Saudi-Egyptian talks toward ending the civil war. However, under Lyndon Johnson things spiraled downward. In late 1964, Egyptians and Americans found themselves on opposite sides of the struggle in the Congo; Egypt sent Soviet arms to the embattled regime of Patrice Lumamba, the United States lent assistance to his opponents. When Nasser's government reputedly allowed a mob to burn down the American cultural center in Cairo, the United States threatened to cut economic aid. Nasser responded defiantly, telling the Americans to "drink from the sea." By late 1965, he was more conciliatory. The Americans responded favorably to the appointment of Zakariya Muhyi al-Din as prime minister in September and renegotiated a new economic package in January 1966. The amity proved, perhaps inevitably, fleeting. The Syrian *coup* of February 1966, the toppling of Nkrumah in Ghana and Sukarno in Indonesia, the murder of Salah Maqlad and the announcement of American arms sales to Saudi Arabia and Israel put Nasser in a defensive mood. The Egyptian President adopted a heightened rhetoric of socialism and revolution and spoke more favorably about the Soviet Union, toward which he now turned for economic and military assistance.

The prelude to the 1967 war began in late 1966, on the eastern front of the Arab-Israeli conflict. In early November, Egypt and Syria signed a defensive alliance, on Nasser's part an attempt to contain Syria's aggressive posture and reduce the odds of escalation. Nine days later, on 13 November, Israel staged a surprise raid against the Jordanian village of Sammu, during which the Jordanian Army suffered heavy casualties with fifteen killed and fifty-four wounded. The Israelis hoped to press King Husayn to act with greater vigilance against Palestinian infiltrators but violent demonstrations by Palestinians in Jordan were more immediate dangers for the King. The UN Security Council, while recognizing that Israel had been provoked, deemed the retaliation excessive and unjustified. The consequence came at a meeting of the unified Arab Defense Council in December, when Jordanian and other Arab representatives pressed Egypt to take the lead in liberating Palestine. Nasser, in turn, challenged the Hashemite King to allow Egyptian, Syrian and Iraqi forces to move freely on Jordanian soil.

In the first months of 1967, Palestinian guerilla attacks from Jordan and Syria into Israel and confrontations between Israeli and Syrian border forces jumped noticeably. One such engagement, on 7 April, turned into a major fight, involving fighter planes from both sides. The Israelis shot down six Syrian jets, then triumphantly "buzzed" Damascus. Syria became particularly volatile. In late April, a Syrian military magazine attacked religion, including Islam, as an impediment to progress. On two successive Fridays, the day of communal prayer, preachers delivering the noon sermon denounced the Ba'thist regime as atheistic, sparking massive demonstrations and a brief general strike. Religious officials in Jordan and Lebanon joined the chorus of critics. The army sentenced the individuals responsible for the offensive article to life imprisonment but the regime, on the defensive, resorted to counter-attacks against imperialist conspiracies and raised the specter of an Israeli attack.

Emotions ran high on all sides. Nasser sent his air force commander and prime minister to Damascus for consultation. Palestinian guerilla activity escalated in early May. Israeli leaders threatened further retaliatory action and a series of statements before Israel's Independence Day celebrations implied a full-scale invasion of Syria. On 13 May, Soviet officials told Anwar al-Sadat in Moscow that Israeli troop movements on the Syrian front indicated an imminent attack. Soviet officials in Cairo passed similar information to Egypt's foreign minister and intelligence chief and, concurrently, warned the Israelis to pull back. Why the Soviets floated such patently false information – few doubt they knew it to be so – remains clouded in hypotheses and conspiracy theories. Taken at face value by the Egyptians, the messages aggravated a febrile crisis. A day later, Egypt began repositioning troops in the Sinai.

On 16 May, Nasser's government formally requested that UNEF forces pull back from their positions in Gaza and the Sinai. The apparent haste with which the UN complied has remained controversial and reflects but one aspect of an inflammatory situation that rapidly spun out of anyone's control. In the original communication, Egypt's Chief of Staff, Muhammad Fawzi, asked only for a limited redeployment, a pull-back from international boundaries at certain positions. The UNEF commander passed the request to the Secretary General, U Thant. Acting against the advice of legal counsel, who urged him to bring the matter before the UN, the Secretary General informed the Egyptians that he judged a partial withdrawal unacceptable. U Thant later explained that he considered the integrity of the organization to be at stake; his lead general dubbed the decision a "blunder." [10] Nasser responded on 18 May, demanding full withdrawal of UNEF forces. After that, the rush to war was unavoidable.

Privately, Nasser still spoke of defusing the crisis. He took care to assert that when he threatened force, such as when he proclaimed Egypt's readiness to restore the pre-1948 *status quo*, he spoke in defensive terms. In other Arab capitals, and in the Cairo press, the rhetoric grew increasingly combative. Between 18 and 24 May Iraq, Saudi Arabia, Jordan and the Palestine Liberation Organization proclaimed their readiness for war. For nearly a week, Nasser refrained from taking the steps that were probably, by then, inevitable. On 22 May, he ordered Egyptian troops to occupy Sharm al-Sheikh and proclaimed the Tiran Straits closed to Israeli, or Israel-bound, shipping. Attempts to retain a defensive posture proved meaningless.

To the Israelis, closing the straits was an act of war. Crippled by a split between those promoting immediate military action and those favoring diplomacy, the cabinet of Prime Minister Levi Eshkol watched and debated. On 28 May, the Israeli government narrowly voted to await the outcome of negotiations. Developments during the following two days tipped the balance. On 30 May, in a move that reportedly caught Nasser by surprise, King Husayn traveled to Cairo to sign a joint defense agreement with Egypt. In the presence of Ahmad al-Shuqayri, a bitter antagonist, the King announced his willingness to welcome Iraqi troops on to his soil. On 1 June, the Israelis formed a national unity government which included

[10] Indar Jit Rikhye, *The Sinai blunder* (London: Frank Cass, 1980).

leading opposition figures. Moshe Dayan, the military hero of Suez and a leading proponent of a pre-emptive war, took the defense portfolio hitherto held by Prime Minister Eshkol, who had consistently promoted diplomacy. The question of whether to see through negotiations or strike first remained on the table until 4 June. On that day, Nasser announced he would send Zakariya Muhyi al-Din to Washington and welcome the American vice-president, Hubert Humphrey, in Cairo. Simultaneously, Iraq joined the Egyptian-Jordanian defense alliance and other non-frontline states – Algeria, Libya, the Sudan and Kuwait – reportedly began mobilizing troops to join the coalition. Israeli hawks pushed for immediate action, while doves, like Foreign Minister Abba Eban, came to agree that a negotiated solution would produce an unacceptable diplomatic victory for Nasser.

In the meantime, Nasser had rejected the advice of his military leaders to initiate combat against the Israelis. His forbearance, as well as his trust in the capability of his armed forces, proved disastrous.

RUINS: 1967–1970

Oh, my heart – don't ask where the passion has gone,
It was a pantheon of my imagination and has collapsed.
Draw drink and imbibe amidst the ruins,
And narrate the tale for me until the tears overflow …
[*Al-Atlal* (The Ruins), 1966]

Egyptian and Arab political leaders and intellectuals referred
to the June 1967 Arab-Israeli war as the "setback" (*al-naksa*). This distinguished it from the 1948 "catastrophe"
(*al-nakba*), although June 1967 was equally, if not more, cata-strophic. Generically, it became known in Arab historiography
as the June War, in tacit defiance of its more popular, semi-biblical, international designation, the Six-Day War, inspired
by the shock and awe of the victors' swift sword and, perhaps,
in the grim recognition that for Egypt, for all intents and pur-poses, the war really ended within a matter of hours.

For Egypt and Nasser, the "setback" manifested itself in all
spheres of public life. The rapidity of the collapse of Egypt's
(and other Arab) armed forces revealed the shaky foundations
of the entire Nasserist revolutionary enterprise. A country
grown restless, under increased police surveillance amidst the
spectacles of military parades and socialist holidays, watching
pendulum tilts toward East and West and suffering the pulsating
acrimony of the "Arab Cold War," had listened for nearly a week
to hyperbolic reports of mythical victories on Nasser's radio

stations. Those who had lived through the "catastrophe," when similar reports trumpeted triumph, perhaps suspended their disbelief. When it was all over, very little remained standing. The Syrian poet of lyrical love, Nizar al-Qabbani, addressed the lies directly. His *Notes on the Margins* reads like graffiti scrawled hastily on palace walls:

> O Sultan, your majesty,
> Because I approached your deaf walls,
> Hoping to reveal my sadness and my plight,
> I was beaten with my shoes.
> Your soldiers forced this shame upon me ...
> If I were promised safety
> From the soldiers of the Sultan,
> I would say to him: you have lost the war twice
> Because you have abandoned the cause of man.[1]

When the "Star of the East," Umm Kulthum, sang more veiled, lyrical lines in *al-Atlal*, a haunting song of lost love inspired by pre-Islamic odes, her Arab audience understood, wept, roared approval and pleaded along with her:

> Give me my freedom, unbind my hands,
> I have given all, held back nothing.
> Oh, your chains cause my wrists to bleed,
> Why do I keep them – why do I accept this?
> Til when shall I remain captive,
> When I could have all the world?

Playing to packed houses throughout the Arab world and in a memorable concert in Paris, the singer raised over a million Egyptian pounds, which she donated to the state to rebuild its armed forces. The crowds pitched in but their trust in their leader, let alone their love for him, would never again be so unconditional.

---

[1] 'What value has the people whose tongue is tied?' in Mounah A. Khoury and Hamid Algar (eds), *An anthology of modern Arabic poetry* (Berkeley: University of California Press, 1974), p. 189.

STAYING ON

The Israeli attack began around 8AM on Monday, 5 June, with massive air strikes against Egyptian airfields and co-ordinated armored attacks against positions in Gaza and the Sinai. Within three hours, the Egyptian air force had been destroyed; by the end of the day Israeli ground forces had pushed through Rafah, cut off Gaza and advanced along the northern Sinai coast as far as El Arish. Learning of the attack on Egypt, Syria immediately began shelling Israeli settlements under the Golan Heights; within two to three hours, Jordanian artillery units also began bombarding Israel. By midday, the Israeli air force had turned its attention to the eastern front and secured command of the sky over Jordan and Syria. Israeli forces then entered the Jordanian-held West Bank. The next day, 6 June, Israeli forces pushed into Arab Jerusalem, toward the Suez Canal and moved to cut off the mountain passes in central Sinai. By the end of 7 June, they had secured the passes, reached Sharm al-Sheikh, over-run the West Bank, reached the Jordan River and captured the old city of Jerusalem. Late on 8 June, first Jordan, then Egypt agreed to ceasefires, while Israel concentrated its forces against Syrian positions on the Golan Heights. On Saturday, 10 June, Syria withdrew from Quneitra, on the crest of the Heights, and Israel agreed to a ceasefire. The war ended with Israeli troops on the Suez Canal, at the Tiran Straits, on the banks of the Jordan River, in control of the West Bank and Jerusalem and atop the Golan.

For Egypt, which lost eighty percent of its armed forces and suffered more than eleven thousand battlefield deaths, the war lasted only four days. On the evening of 9 June, Nasser delivered what proved to be his last great address to the nation. Speaking on radio and television, he assumed full responsibility for the defeat and announced his resignation. Shades of 1956 colored his account. Egypt had, he stubbornly insisted, confronted not only Israel but also the superpowers and had refrained from initiating war at the urgent request of the Soviet

Ambassador, on 26 May. When hostilities did begin, the degree of "imperialist collusion" had become apparent: British aircraft had participated in air strikes, Nasser asserted, and American planes had reconnoitered Egyptian positions.

As Nasser, and the nation, confronted the scale and rapidity of the military collapse, the traditional defiant tone was missing. Seated in front of a plain curtain, the *Rayyis* was haggard, physically and emotionally drained. His exhausted eyes frequently glanced down at his prepared text. All had not been lost, he assured his people. The urgent tasks ahead of them included studying the lessons of the setback and acting to reverse course and "remove the traces of aggression against us." Nasser announced his readiness to "return to the ranks of the masses and do my duty with them like every other citizen," The "forces of imperialism" would claim that Nasser, not the Egyptian people, is their enemy, he asserted. His response echoed the famous words he shouted thirteen years earlier, in October 1954, after the attempt on his life: "If Abd al-Nasser dies, each of you is Abd al-Nasser."

> The aspiration for Arab unity began before Abd al-Nasser
> and will remain after Abd al-Nasser. I always used to tell you
> that the nation remains and that the individual – whatever
> his role and however great his contribution to the causes of
> his homeland – is only a tool of the popular will and not its
> creator.[2]

Zakariya Muhyi al-Din, a Free Officer comrade and former prime minister (and, not incidentally, a man viewed with favor in the West) succeeded him.

An explosion followed, as millions of Egyptians poured into the streets, calling upon Nasser to stay, not to abandon them. Cynics suggested a masterful staging, recalling the collective resignation of the RCC in March 1954, when Liberation Rally

---

[2] Walter Laqueur (ed.), *The Israel–Arab reader* (New York: Bantam, 1969), pp. 192–3.

members clearly provoked massive street demonstrations on behalf of the officers against Muhammad Nagib. Now, facing the reality of defeat – with all that this entailed – Egyptians needed no prompting. Their cries and tears may have reflected the weakness of the political order or, as some would say later, the intoxicating facade of progress. At the same time they show, just as if not more clearly, the populist power of the leader. In the emotional fury of the moment, Egyptians could see no alternative but perseverance under his command. Nasser, who had never before wavered in his self-identity as a leader, accepted the referendum of the streets. He announced he would stay in office; together he and his people would begin the process of rebuilding.

The legions who called Nasser back also demanded to know what had gone so terribly wrong. Most fingers pointed at the military, a logical target, but broader questions remained, many of them never definitively answered. If, as most accept, Egypt did not want war, why had it gone to such lengths to provoke the Israelis? Did Nasser trust that his armed forces could, if need be, defeat the enemy? What role had the superpowers, particularly the Soviet Union with its blatantly false intelligence, played in escalating tensions? To what extent did Nasser sense the immediacy of an Israeli strike, and to what extent did he recognize the scale of defeat in the opening phase of the war?

Answers to these questions have to account for the extent to which the military, always a political force in Nasserist Egypt, had become the personal fiefdom of Nasser's erstwhile comrade, Abd al-Hakim Amr, particularly in the aftermath of their 1962 showdown. When, in 1964, Amr became Vice-President for Military Affairs, he restructured his command in such a way that Nasser loyalists, up to and including the chief of staff, were kept out of power. Amr, who had assured Nasser that the Yemen operation would be easy, over-estimated the organizational and fighting ability of his troops and at times seems to have either disregarded or overtly remanded orders from his president. As war clouds gathered, he appeared to be itching for a showdown with the Israelis, especially for a rematch with his personal nemesis, Moshe Dayan, and promoted the idea of an Egyptian first strike.

Nasser's apparent trust in Amr and the military, after the power struggles and the Yemen débâcle, can only be understood as a product of the uncertainty as to who exercised real power in the country. His actions and words emphasized the extent to which he saw Egypt's pre-war maneuvering as purely political. His rhetoric was designed to defuse bellicose challenges to his leadership of the Arab world, particularly from Syria where, by mid-May, the situation was highly explosive. With Israel threatening dramatic action and Soviet intelligence overstating the immediacy of an attack, Nasser felt compelled to act. When U Thant rejected a partial redeployment of the UNEF, the Egyptian leader pushed things to the brink; he did so again when he blocked the Tiran Straits. Nasser expected war, but insisted Egypt would not initiate armed conflict. When Shams Badran, his War Minister (and an Amr ally) passed on the Soviet Premier Alexi Kosygin's promise to support the Arabs, an Egyptian diplomat discounted the promise as "normal Russian expressions while tossing back vodka" but Radio Cairo reported a highly-embellished version.[3] On 2 June, Nasser told his high command to expect an Israeli attack within forty-eight to seventy-two hours, by 5 June at the latest. Yet he presumably trusted that American pressure on Israel, buoyed by Soviet pronouncements, might tilt the scales in favor of diplomacy.

The behavior of Egypt's political and military leaders on the eve of war reveals a dangerous separation from reality. Nasser spoke at a ceremony marking Iraq's entry into the defensive alliance and threatened to use force against any ship breaching the Red Sea blockade. Amr was at a party until well into the

[3] Michael B. Oren, *Six days of war: June 1967 and the making of the modern Middle East* (New York: Ballantine, 2002), p. 125.

early morning hours, the chief of ground forces was on leave in Ismailia and the air force commander at a daughter's wedding. So when, around midnight, the first reports of Israeli troop movements around Gaza and Rafah trickled in, no one of import was present to read them. The general staff awaited Amr's arrival at an air base for a morning flight tour of positions. The Israeli attack caught them in the air, out of radio contact for ninety minutes, which undoubtedly contributed to the inability of the Egyptian air force to muster any resistance to the Israeli sorties. Most accounts agree that Nasser only learned of the true extent of the disaster late in the afternoon of 5 June. On day two he apparently tried, without success, to countermand Amr's order for units to retreat. A week later, with hostilities ended, the time to start settling accounts had arrived.

BROTHERS DIVIDED

Despite lofty talk about eliminating "traces of aggression," the magnitude of what had happened engulfed Egypt and the Arab world. Arab politics, noted Malcolm Kerr, an astute, sympathetic observer, "have ceased to be fun."[4] An era in which, for all the acrimonious, rhetorical, hyperbole amongst rivals, a sense of buoyant optimism had prevailed, had passed. Nasser hesitated to attend the Arab summit in Khartoum in August 1967, fearful of political defeat, wary of confronting "the gloating of those I stood against throughout the Arab homeland" and "afraid to face the ordinary man in the street."[5] In the end he did go – and was greeted by raucous, adoring, crowds. According to Abd al-Magid Farid, Secretary General of the Egyptian

---

[4] Malcolm H. Kerr, *The Arab Cold War: Gamal Abd al-Nasir and his rivals* (London: Oxford University Press, 1972), p.v.
[5] Abdel Magid Farid, *Nasser: The final years* (Reading: Ithaca Press, 1994), p. 53.

presidency, Sudanese officials asked Nasser's plane to circle to allow King Faysal to land ahead of him, fearing that if Nasser disembarked first there would be no one left to greet the Saudi monarch.

At the Khartoum summit, Arab leaders propounded the three infamous "no"s regarding relations with Israel: no formal

Statecraft. Nasser is greeted in Rabat by the Moroccan monarch, Hasan II, in December 1969 on the occasion of the Conference of Arab States. Between the two leaders, in the background, smiling, is PLO chairman Yasser Arafat. (Property of the author.)

peace, no negotiations and no recognition. However, deep fault lines lay beneath the smooth facade of rejectionist unity. Nasser, King Faysal and King Husayn emphasized their inability to and the inadvisability of undertaking military action against Israel. They needed to rebuild both military strength and political legitimacy. This implied the recognition of certain realities, chiefly that indirect talks, as much if not more than armed conflict, might pave the way towards the return of lost territory and perhaps some resolution of the long-standing conflict with the Zionist state. The prime target of those counseling restraint was the PLO Chairman, Ahmad al-Shuqayri, who was at times openly scorned. His dismissal by leading Arab heads of state, as well as the enormity of the tragedy for Palestinians in the Israeli-occupied territories and front-line Arab states, precipitated his demise, the rise of Yasser Arafat, leader of the Fatah movement and the ascendancy of other Palestinian militias.

For the moment, Nasser knew the business in hand well. To rebuild confidence in his broader socio-political agenda, the Arab socialist revolution, he needed first to assess the state of his armed forces and the degree to which he could exert authority over them. Rearming would prove to be the easy part. Within a week of the June War's end, Nasser was promised assistance by the Soviets; within days of the message the Soviet President, Nikolai Podgorny, visited Cairo. By the following spring, Nasser could claim that Egypt's defenses had been rebuilt. Yet, in the immediate aftermath of the disaster, he faced resounding calls to hold accountable those responsible for the military's performance. As early as 8 June, when the truth of the war's course became public, throngs of Egyptians took to the streets calling for him to oust the "incompetents." This meant, ultimately, cracking Abd al-Hakim Amr's bastion of power.

Amr did not go quietly. The Field Marshal blamed Nasser for not initiating war with Israel in late May and felt personally betrayed. When Nasser retracted his own resignation after his 9 June address, he did not reinstate Amr. On 10 June, Amr barricaded himself in one of his Cairo villas, surrounded by loyal units from where he despatched a series of bulletins calling for political reform. In response to this as much as to public sentiment, Nasser ordered Amr and fifty top commanders to be cashiered. Confronted with the prospects of a mutiny, on 11 June he set up a special commission to investigate questions of fault and announced that Amr would stay on as Vice President. Ten days later, Nasser assumed the post of Prime Minister and appointed Zakariya Muhyi al-Din and Husayn al-Shafi'i as deputies. Nasser had lured Amr out of his seclusion with a dinner invitation. Afterwards, the Field Marshal found himself escorted home and placed under house arrest. On 23 July 1967, the fifteenth anniversary of the Revolution, Nasser addressed the "most serious crisis we have faced in the history of our revolutionary work." Egyptians confronted a "savage conspiracy" against which he would serve as "their representative" in a "struggle not dependent on any individual." [6]

On 4 September, the government announced the arrest of Amr, Shams Badran, Salah Nasr and other leading military and intelligence figures. They were charged with plotting to force Nasser to reinstate Amr as commander of the military and to drop the investigation into complicity in the defeat. The drama played itself out a week later, in circumstances that remain cloaked in controversy. According to official accounts, on 13 September Amr attempted suicide by taking cyanide. He was taken to hospital but, two days later, swallowed an additional capsule that he had managed to keep in his possession (or, according to some, that he had been allowed to retain). Nasser insisted that Amr's death was "even more cruel for me than the defeat." [7] The Field Marshal's fiercest defenders still insist he was murdered. The unraveling of the relationship between Nasser and Amr, bosom buddies of opposite temperament, remains the stuff of legend, epic-mythic and tabloid-sensation-

[6] Lacqueur, *Israel-Arab reader*, pp. 197–204.
[7] Lacouture, *Nasser*, p. 317.

alist. Booksellers in Cairo still stock exposés of Amr's indiscretions – his secret marriages and his various addictions – and the latest "revelations" of Nasser's "plot" to eliminate his rival.

SHIFTING SANDS

Nasser and his aides moved to address the growing popular outcry against the authoritarian face of the regime. Many of those clamoring for greater liberties did so not in the name of rebellion but in the cause of restoring the revolution to its proper course, taking aim at those privileged people who benefited from bureaucratic inertia and military and party privilege. Amr's chief associates faced a special military tribunal in January 1968 and in March, Shams Badran, Salah Nasr and several others received life sentences and a further thirty-two were sentenced to harsh prison terms. In February, light sentences handed down to the air force commander and other senior field officers had sparked unprecedented riots led by students and workers chanting "No leniency for the traitors" and "No socialism without freedom." Nasser shuffled his government and, on 30 March, promised greater personal and political freedoms. Reasserting a commitment to socialism, he announced free elections within the ASU – although not yet true political parties. A referendum in early May approved the initiative, and an elected national congress met in September to select a new central committee. However, against the spirit of Nasser's decree, ASU insiders nominated its members. Nasser professed dismay at the process but few saw this as anything other than a weak apology for his unwillingness truly to reform the political system.

Unfulfilled promises exacerbated Nasser's domestic troubles. In November 1968, protests over changes in the examination system spread from theology students in Mansura to the broader student body in Alexandria. When Israeli jets flew uncontested over Nag Hammadi, bombing an electrical installation, demonstrations erupted in Upper Egypt, centered on Assiut University. By this time, the protesters' agenda encompassed civil liberties and greater activism against the Israelis. Crowds called for the head of Nasser's Interior Minister, Sha'rawi Gum'a, and some even suggested the *Rayyis* resign. The most widespread demonstrations since 1954 resulted in five hundred arrests. Nasser denounced "counter-revolutionary" tendencies incited by an "irresponsible minority." [8] A series of conspiracy trials followed, one relating to a supposed assassination plot. In January 1969, elections for a new National Assembly returned twenty-seven percent of incumbents but the percentage of independents still remained strikingly low. In July, in conjunction with the Revolution's sixteenth anniversary, the government announced a new phase of land reform, with the limits on ownership lowered to fifty *feddans* per individual. Increasingly, however, newly expropriated land was channeled not to peasants but to state agricultural companies.

A national debate about the future took place in the halls of government, in the press, on campuses, in cafes and at rural cooperatives. The left continued to decry the inevitable failings of half-hearted or surface socialism. Liberal economists and intellectuals favored a more open political process, bolstered by foreign investment, relaxed restrictions on private capital and, above all, austerity measures. A centrist tendency looked to purging corrupt, incompetent or obstructive elements within the ASU, bureaucracy, military and intelligence services. Finally, a resurgent Islamist movement, rooted in the Muslim Brotherhood but led by younger, more radical initiates, emphasized the misguided secular orientation of the Nasserist state.

In a period of such national malaise, at best open debate provided a spark of optimism; at worst it represented a safety valve to diminish the risks of mass politics. Beyond the press, some excitement was generated in the arts, where leading writers, dramatists and filmmakers, often in cooperation with

[8] Stephens, *Nasser*, p. 537.

state censors, seized upon new-found opportunities for more pointed social and political criticism. The majority of movies remained popular entertainments – comedies, police dramas and melodramas – but a small number of films, made by leading directors and featuring major stars, captured audiences. The most celebrated, a 1968 adaptation of Nagib Mahfouz's novel *Miramar*, boldly treated careerism in the ASU as symptomatic of broader socio-political corruption. In dialogue more pointed than that of the novel, two old *regimistes*, a liberal intellectual and a former high government official whose political rights had been stripped and property sequestered, speak fondly of the good old days and mock the promises of the July Revolution. Even comedies took a political turn. In *Ard al-nifaq* (Land of Hypocrisy), starring popular comic Fuad al-Muhandis, a special "hypocrisy elixir" cooked up by a wizardly pharmacist helps a pitiful low-grade bureaucrat climb the ladder of success until, by mistake, he imbibes a truth potion and winds up back where he started, on the bottom rung. The wizard disappears, having closed his shop due to "lack of public morality."

The June War and its aftermath took their toll on the President. Nearly a year later, in April 1968, he compared himself to "a man walking in a desert surrounded by moving sands not knowing whether, if he moved, he would be swallowed up by the sands or would find the right path." [9] Nasser had been suffering from diabetes since the late fifties. He still ate healthily but chain-smoked and took little exercise. In the summer of 1968, after collapsing from overwork and stress, complicated by arteriolosclerosis in his upper legs, he traveled to the Soviet Union for treatment. By mid-1969, after the political upheaval had subsided, Nasser had quit smoking – his only luxury, he complained – and appeared to have regained his health. Few, including his wife Tahiya, were aware that an extended six-week vacation in September 1969 followed a heart attack that left him hugely incapacitated. Soviet physicians repeated his personal

[9] Stephens, *Nasser*, p. 510.

doctors' warnings to reduce his workload. According to his confidant, Muhammad Hasanayn Haykal, he twice considered resigning. Unwilling to reveal the true state of his health, Nasser feared that a retreat from active politics would be considered political surrender. And so, until the end, it was all or nothing.

ATTRITION

Domestic politics – guided by popular calls to correct or rebuild the Revolution – were played against the backdrop of regional affairs. The "consequences of aggression" dominated Nasser's attention and, arguably, killed him. Egypt faced myriad difficult tasks in the regional and international arenas: rearmament, the reconstruction of defenses, the restoration of morale in the ranks and a diplomacy that emphasized the continuing battle while restraining precipitate calls to arms. Chastened, well aware of the errors of May 1967, Nasser would not follow others' lead nor bow to their goading again.

When Nikolai Podgorny visited Egypt in mid-June, he was accompanied by Marshal Zakharov, the Soviet Chief of Staff. Scornful of the ease with which Egypt had squandered its Russian military hardware, the Marshal emphasized training over rearmament. Egypt proposed, and received, fifteen hundred brigade-level advisers. Zakharov remained in Egypt – Nasser jokingly referred to it as house arrest – until November, when he declared the defenses ready. Soviet military assistance was complemented, in the early autumn, by financial aid from oil-rich Gulf states. At Khartoum, Nasser and King Faysal had finalized arrangements to end the Yemen conflict and the Saudi King promoted Egypt's cause to the tune of $250 million. A series of diplomatic visits by Arab leaders – King Husayn of Jordan, Iraq's Abd al-Rahman Arif (whose brother, Abd al-Salam, had died in a helicopter crash in April 1966) and Libya's Mu'ammar al-Qadhafi – reinforced Cairo's standing as the Arab "capital." Emboldened by these commitments, Nasser proceeded with reshuffling the high command. His new War Minister, Muhammad Fawzi, who had at first been wary of removing Amr's portrait from his office, oversaw the purge of one thousand officers. Restoring a sense of purpose for men in uniform proved trickier. Fawzi admitted later that public pressure, more than military readiness, prompted the slogan "what was taken by force can only be recovered by force" and a future Chief of Staff, Sa'd al-Din al-Shadhli, recalled that anyone in uniform faced ridicule in the streets and morale "fell to near-suicidal levels." [10]

Despite a growing inclination to seek a negotiated resolution of the Arab-Israeli conflict, Nasser determined to embark upon limited military engagement with Israel along the Sinai front.

The War of Attrition, rooted in delusions of Arab demographic advantages, cost the Egyptians far more than it did the Israelis and did little for either civilian or military morale. It did, however, advance Nasser's diplomatic agenda, by drawing the attention of the superpowers to the dangers of real war in the region and hastening a more even-handed initiative by the United States.

Small-scale hostilities along the Suez Canal, blocked, as in 1956, to nautical passage, erupted within weeks of the 10 June 1967 ceasefire. On 1 July, an Israeli raid, a reprisal for a series of Egyptian ambushes, resulted in a pitched battle on the Egyptian side of the Canal. Ten days later, both sides agreed to the establishment of UN observer posts. A series of dogfights followed but gradually normality was restored. Israeli and Egyptian troops eyed each other cautiously, but exchanged pleasantries as they fished from their opposite banks. In September, the shooting resumed and in October, Egyptian missiles sank the Israeli destroyer *Eilat* in the Mediterranean off Port Said. Israel responded with a massive barrage across the Canal, prompting the evacuation of major cities — four hundred thousand refugees left Port Said, Ismailia and Suez — and Nasser

---

[10] Yoram Meital, *Eygpt's struggle for peace: Continuity and change, 1967–1977* (Gainesville: Florida University Press, 1997), p. 16.

to order aggressive actions to cease. A year later, in September 1968, with 150,000 troops in the Canal Zone, he opened a new phase of the struggle, ordering Egyptian batteries along key stretches of the Canal to open fire simultaneously. Commando raids accompanied further barrages. The Israelis responded with a raid deep into Upper Egypt which destroyed a series of bridges and a transformer station. Egypt halted to take stock, while the Israelis began construction of the Bar-Lev Line, a controversial series of defensive fortifications and observation posts along the Canal's east bank.

Nasser proclaimed the official War of Attrition the following spring. Artillery bombardments, dogfights and cross-canal forays continued without respite from April 1969 until August 1970. Casualties mounted on both sides, but Israeli ground and air raids in and around Egyptian population centers undercut rhetoric of the war's "liberation" phase. In July 1969, Israel unleashed its "flying artillery." sending out a thousand sorties over Egypt in two months (compared to Egypt's hundred). A series of high-profile commando operations in the fall – in the most infamous Israeli raiders carried off an entire radar station – emphasized Israel's control of the skies. By the start of the new year, the Israelis had destroyed most of Egypt's air defenses and begun bombing military installations near Cairo.

Nasser kept in close contact with the Soviets throughout, although concerns about his health distracted him from military matters. When he traveled to Moscow in July 1968, his Soviet doctors scheduled him to return for treatment after Revolution Day. Only his closest advisors – Muhammad Hasanayn Haykal, Anwar al-Sadat and Abd al-Mun'im Riyad – knew the severity of his condition. His first heart attack, in September 1968, kept him at home and temporarily out of commission, although not for as long as his Soviet physician advised. On 22 January 1970, he returned secretly to Moscow where he pressed the Soviets to supply Egypt with the most advanced surface-to-air missile installations. At a hastily arranged Politburo meeting, the Soviets acceded reluctantly to Nasser's request for Soviet teams to operate the equipment while training Egyptian crews. In April 1970, materials and technicians arrived in Egypt, together with Soviet pilots to patrol the skies. In response, Israel ceased flying deep-penetration raids. Fighting remained intense along the Canal Zone, although by mid-summer Soviet-monitored defenses, deployed closer to the front lines, began to undercut Israeli air superiority.

The Egyptians had begun to consider seriously a series of US and UN initiatives designed to promote a comprehensive peace. In December 1969, the American Secretary of State, William Rogers, proposed an Israeli withdrawal commensurate with UN Resolution 242 (adopted 22 November 1967) in return for formal peace. Rogers first unveiled plans for a bilateral Egyptian-Israeli solution, followed by a similar arrangement for Jordan. The Rogers Plan stalled, receiving little support in any quarter. In April, Assistant Secretary of State Joseph Sisco visited Cairo. Four days earlier, Israeli bombers had struck a school in the Delta, killing fifty children. Nasser emphasized Egypt's bitterness at the American-Israeli relationship yet, in his May Day address, he made overtures to the United States and on 25 June Rogers proposed a limited ceasefire. Four days later Nasser traveled to Moscow where he stayed for nineteen days, mostly to rest and on his way home informed his hosts that he would accept the American proposal. Egypt needed a respite in which to complete its missile defenses, he argued, and Israel would accept a ceasefire only under American auspices. Nasser announced Egypt's acceptance of the Rogers Plan publicly on Revolution Day. On 7 August, as the hour of the ceasefire approached, the Egyptians clumsily assembled dummy installations to camouflage work that broke the strict terms of the agreement. Consequently, US-brokered negotiations to move beyond a ceasefire fell through. Within a month, another front had exploded, an Arab civil war on Jordanian soil, between King Husayn and Palestinian militias, which threatened to engulf the region.

RACE AGAINST DEATH

Jordan, simmering since the end of the June War, came to a rapid boil in August 1970. A quarter of a million new refugees from the West Bank had found themselves homeless in Husayn's kingdom. The young amongst them became foot soldiers for a radicalized PLO, dominated by Yasser Arafat's Fatah movement but comprising a variety of rival factions, many of which promoted a more militant stance on behalf of a nationalist and, in some cases, a broader social revolution. Having lost faith in the ability, or even will, of the Arab states to act on their behalf, the *fidayin* constructed a network of armed camps, from which they regularly carried out raids against Israel. The most radical organizations refused to collaborate formally with the PLO; in July 1968, in response, the Palestine National Council, the legislative branch of the national movement, amended the PLO Charter to advocate armed struggle as the sole path to liberation. Between September 1969 and early summer of 1970, the Popular Front for the Liberation of Palestine (PFLP) and Popular Democratic Front (PDF, formerly the PDFLP) allied with the Palestine National Council to form an Armed Struggle Command.

Headquartered in Amman, with bases spread along the frontier with Israel, the PLO presented an increasingly explicit challenge to Hashemite sovereignty. Nearly half the commando raids into Israel originated in Jordan. Palestinian guerillas ran the refugee camps and armed fighters patrolled the capital and other cities, controlling traffic, stopping people to check identification and symbolically demonstrating a presence that defied state authority. On occasion, King Husayn sent troops into the camps to assert his power. A showdown grew imminent. The king warned that if he accepted the Rogers plan – which he did in July 1970 – armed clashes would increase. On 20 August, he flew to Cairo for consultation. Nasser warned him against attacking the Palestinians. The Jordanians might crush the *fidayin*, he cautioned, but this would mean slaughter, leaving Husayn to rule "a kingdom of ghosts." [11] Four days later, Nasser counseled Yasser Arafat that, however legitimate the Palestinian grievances against Husayn, his people stood to gain far more through co-existence and to lose everything through confrontation. The danger point seemed to pass, and Nasser left for a month-long holiday, under orders to rest completely, at the Mediterranean resort city, Mersa Matruh.

The flurry of events that precipitated what the Palestinians dub "Black September" quashed Nasser's vacation plans. In early September, scattered fighting broke out in Amman and northern Jordan between Hashemite forces and Palestinian militias. The country was hovering on the brink of civil war when, on 6 September, PFLP guerillas hijacked four international flights. They diverted one plane to Cairo, which, after allowing crew and passengers to disembark, they blew up. Israeli security guards aboard an El Al flight foiled a second hijack attempt, killing one guerilla and overpowering another. The other two planes landed at a remote Jordanian airstrip from where the hijackers demanded the release of comrades jailed in Europe. On 9 September, a fifth hijacked airliner landed. Negotiations ensued, under the auspices of the International Red Cross but with Nasser playing a crucial background role. Eventually, the three hundred hostages were released in exchange for prisoners. The guerillas, who had named the airstrip "Liberation Airport," went on to seize control of a nearby oil refinery.

The PLO had denounced the hijackings but, sensing the inevitability of widespread combat, Yasser Arafat formed a unified high command. On 16 September, King Husayn appointed a military government; a day later he ordered a full-scale assault against Palestinian bases, refugee camps and the PLO headquarters in Amman. Fierce fighting raged for eleven days. Palestinian

[11] Mohamed Heikal, *The road to Ramadan* (London: Quadrangle, 1975), p. 97.

casualties, fighters and non-combatants, reached thousands. On 21 September, Syria moved tank columns across the border to assist the PLO but Syrian leaders, divided on the wisdom of the incursion, quickly withdrew them, in the face of Israeli threats to intervene on behalf of King Husayn. With disaster looming, Nasser called Arab leaders to an emergency meeting in Cairo. They arrived between 22 and 24 September.

Animosity pervaded the gathering. Arafat and Husayn arrived carrying pistols and surrendered them only reluctantly before entering the Nile Hilton, site of the gathering. Each insisted that co-existence was no longer an option. Nasser took personal charge of the negotiations, reminding the antagonists that "there are men, women and children dying. We are in a race with death." [12] On 27 September Husayn and Arafat agreed to a ceasefire and separation of forces, supervised by Arab states.

Nasser, who could not sit for extended periods without excruciating pain, was exhausted. Yet he insisted on seeing each of his guests off at Cairo Airport. Colonel Qadhafi of Libya, who, although unaware of its severity, recognized the extent of his idol's fatigue, attempted to slip away quietly but Nasser chased after him. On 28 September, after bidding farewell to the Emir of Kuwait, Nasser returned home to rest his legs and, hopefully, sleep away the day. He visited his children briefly, then, skipping lunch, retired to his room, asking for a glass of orange juice. He called for his doctors, who determined that he had suffered a second heart attack. Within the hour his closest advisors assembled – Sami Sharaf, Sha'rawi Gum'a, Anwar al-Sadat, Muhammad Fawzi, Muhammad Hasanayn Haykal and Husayn al-Shafi'i. According to Haykal, Nasser's pulse steadied. He spoke of visiting the front before resuming his vacation. He fiddled with the radio, told his doctor he felt better, shut his eyes and died. When the truth had sunk in, they summoned his wife, Tahiya. She sat alone with her husband while the others

[12] Stephens, *Nasser*, p. 554.

called an emergency meeting of the ASU central committee and the cabinet. Word soon spread through Cairo that someone important had died. Many presumed Husayn and Arafat had gone for their pistols. Eventually, Anwar al-Sadat came to the radio station and announced the leader's passing. The shock waves began to radiate.

CONCLUSION:
A PICTURE

A picture – we all want a picture,
A picture – under the banner of victory.
A picture of a joyous people under the banner of victory.
Oh, time past, picture us – we will draw close to each other
    again,
And anyone who keeps his distance from the field of vision will
    never appear in this picture.
[*Sura* (A Picture), 1966]

This book started with a snapshot and lyric from July 1958, the sixth anniversary of the July Revolution, five months into the wary experiment of the United Arab Republic. The conclusion begins with a snapshot and lyric from July 1966, the Revolution's thirteenth anniversary, four years after the collapse of the UAR and one year before the June 1967 "setback." *Sura*, which means picture or photograph, is perhaps the most memorable and fondly recalled anthem of the Nasser era. This favoritism is based primarily on the song's catchy tune – its chorus is easily sung – although if pressed, people with a historical memory will recall it as reflecting the climactic moments of revolutionary socialist enthusiasm, before the fall. Composed by the team that produced the majority of the most popular anthems, Salah Jahin (lyrics) and Kamal al-Tawil (music) and sung – yet again – by Abd al-Halim Hafiz, the Nightingale of the Revolution, *Sura* depicts the new, egalitarian Egypt on the march.

All of us in the picture are colleagues, fulfilling what the
    Charter called for,

From the youngest child in braids, on the farms and in schools,
   moving in sync,
To the peasant, the essence of good and beauty,
To the preacher, guardian of the Qur'an,
To the soldier, the lion, who wears on his shoulders the armor
   of the nation ...
Professors, scientists, factory workers and doctors from the
   working folk.
Men behind their desks serve you with good spirit –
This picture has no slackers sleeping on the job!
It has nothing but the total revolutionary Egyptian Arab
   individual ...

The song ends with an evocation to the leader: "This picture is
completed with pioneers, with Nasser, their hands in his."

Sura, the last of the great nationalist anthems, is also the song
that almost never was. Years later, Kamal al-Tawil recalled how
he tried to avoid the call for yet another number for yet another
Revolution Day gala. An aristocratic child, son of a pasha who
sat in the last *Wafd* government, Tawil embraced the Nasserist
project and set it to music. By 1966 he had lost enthusiasm, not
so much for Nasserist ideology but for the spectacle, which he
felt had become routine. A person of Tawil's stature, however,
did not bow out so easily. Informed that he risked losing his
passport if he failed to co-operate, the composer took up his
pen and produced yet another masterpiece.

The song, literally and figuratively, is a snapshot of an era,
conveying the imagery by which the regime sought to identify
itself. There were other, less laudatory, images, not evoked in
the 1966 anthem or its predecessors, the snapshots either of
those who had never embraced the Nasser regime or those who
had (some less conditionally than others) but then lost faith.

One image might be of a gathering of dispossessed former
aristocrats, still very well off by local standards, gazing out
across a city and country that is no longer theirs, berating
Nasser and his comrades as ill-mannered upstarts and crimi-
nals, who undermined Egypt's sense of civility and brought

the nation to ruin. They might be gazing on scores of dilapidated villas, gardens gone to seed, chandeliers replaced by light bulbs, and walls painted the pale institutional hue of requisitioned government offices. Or the image might be of people who found themselves in Nasser's political prisons, being arrested, perhaps in the middle of the night, perhaps on

Icon. A hand-painted portrait of Nasser outside a café (later an upholstery shop) adjacent to downtown Cairo. (Photograph by the author.)

unfounded suspicions, and driven to an overcrowded military prison on the edge of the desert. Some might recall an image of an undergraduate sitting in an overcrowded university classroom taking notes not on the professor's lecture, but on the conversations of fellow students. Or of the semi-stranger, eavesdropping on an animated conversation in the local café. Islamists, especially, have detailed the brutality of life in Nasser's concentration camps.

Some of the dissenting images are a historical. Bureaucratic listlessness, the anarchic co-mingling of motorists and pedestrians, the official on the make and the internal confidential agent are neither the creation nor the unique product of Nasser's Egypt. Under the monarchy, incarceration of political prisoners had hardly been less brutal, although it must be noted that it was in Nasser's, not Farouk's prisons that Sayyid Qutb came to believe that "the guards and torturers ... had forgotten God" and that only the imprisoned Brothers "were still true Muslims."[1] Then there are the stunning images of June 1967, which cannot be laid at the feet of any other regime: shaken soldiers, their weapons lost or abandoned, staggering across the desert towards home, or sitting cross-legged inside barbed wire containment areas, watched by triumphant enemies; the shocked faces of those at home discovering the truth behind the lies broadcast on state radio, then screaming, refugees from the storm, for their leader to not abandon them.

A year after *Sura* premiered, Egypt had become a very different country. During the first days of the June 1967 war, Egypt's leading musical artists set up recording studios in the basement of the Radio and Television building, where they hastily composed and recorded a string of new battle anthems, most short and quickly forgotten in the aftermath of the "setback."When the artists emerged a week later they, like the rest of the nation, saw how empty even their brilliant tunes had

---

[1] Gilles Kepel, *Muslim extremism in Egypt: Prophet and pharaoh* (Berkeley: University of California Press, 1986), pp. 28–29.

proven. Some endeavored to rally a dispirited nation, none with more energy than Umm Kulthum. However, the songs that moved her audiences all over the Arab world were now sung to broken hearts and shattered dreams.

YOU LIVE!

Three years after the "setback" the leader was gone. When the news was announced, Egyptians again poured into the streets, as they had in June 1967 when Nasser admitted military defeat and announced his resignation. Now, they could not shout for him to stay. They wept, tore their hair, slapped their cheeks. The more stoic carried his official portrait, a black band draped across the top left corner. On the day of his funeral, mourners commandeered the streets and took possession of his coffin from the honor guard. Alexi Kosygin, the Soviet premier, warned his hosts against losing control, but the masses sought solace, not rebellion. "You live, Abu Khalid," they cried, naming Nasser, as was the custom, as the father of his eldest son. They accompanied his body to the mosque where he was interred, in Abbasiya, not far from his home and near the barracks from which the tanks had rumbled in the early morning hours of 23 July, eighteen years before. The public outpouring of grief was not limited to Egypt. In Beirut mourners – and those who were advised to stand allied with the mourners – set tires aflame and decorated cars with black trimming. The scene was played throughout the Arab world.

Some found the sudden transition of power unbelievable. In a familiar anecdote, when Galal Mu`awad, the broadcaster who had so often announced Nasser to radio audiences, introduced his successor for the first time, he lapsed into old habit, announcing him as "al-Za`im al-Khalid (the glorious leader), Gamal Abd al-Nasser." Anwar al-Sadat was not amused and had Mu`awad sacked, but the broadcaster, caught up in the emotion of the moment, had meant no deliberate insult. For nearly two decades, Egypt had known one ruler. Nasser had defined popular aspirations as well as the state's, Arab aspirations as well as the Arab world and, in a wider sphere, the "winds of change" that had swept away colonialism.

Two epitaphs resounded loudest in the immediate aftermath of his death. The first is the notion that he had – symbolically – died in 1967, when the edifice of progress collapsed so suddenly. It soon became a cliché, but it was grounded in the realities of Nasser's declining health, the blow the collapse gave to his morale and, not least, by his falling out with Abd al-Hakim Amr. The second is the idea that he had expended his last energies hoping to save innocent Palestinian lives and had died a "martyr to the cause of Arab brotherhood." [2]

How should one assess his character and career from the distance of decades? Nasser was a man of quiet convictions able, by the force of his personality, to dominate a cohort of contemporaries, dedicated patriots motivated toward some form of political activism. He was an attractive man, tall, bronze-skinned, with a wide but not round face, piercing eyes and an engaging, winning smile. According to most of his early fellow-officers, he was decidedly serious, a listener more than a talker. Yet, as his many photographs show, he enjoyed a hearty laugh and reveled in the approbation of the crowd, whether from a balcony or traveling, always standing, in an open vehicle. He was a reader (when he had the time), an avid film buff, sharing his generation's special affinity for Hollywood as well as for their own "Hollywood on the Nile" and a chess player.

It has often been stated that he was "a tactician rather than a strategist," a leader who tended to "react rather than initiate." [3] That is not the same as saying that he lacked vision or did not carefully plot his actions. His dreams were like those of his contemporaries. The set of principles that became known as Nasserism never constituted a rigid ideology, rather, they

[2] Kerr, *Arab Cold War*, p. 154.
[3] Wheelock, *Nasser's new Egypt*, p. 223.

evolved to meet the challenges, achievements and setbacks of any given time. In retrospect Nasser was not always as careful as he might have been but he rarely acted on impulse. He was not above a bit of calculated grandstanding. Immediately after seizing power, Free Officers insiders debated the fate of the King. When the committee proved deadlocked, with a vocal element favoring trial and execution, Nasser walked out, threatening to resign. At the same time, he preferred to stay in the background, behind the RCC's facade of equality and its figurehead leader, Muhammad Nagib. When a nervous majority voted to execute the labor organizers at Kafr al-Dawwar, he agreed. Arguably, it was his characteristic caution that allowed the Free Officers to avoid suppression in the late 1940s and early 1950s, when so many other dissident organizations, civilian and military, had not.

The "March crisis" of 1954 proved to be a major turning point in his political career. When the public outcry against the RCC paralyzed most of his colleagues, Nasser worked, with a hand-picked coterie, to plot the council's survival. He emerged from the episode as the clear leader of the Revolution. The following October, when he survived the assassination attempt during a public address in Alexandria, he discovered a public persona. Conspiracy theorists persistently assert that the event was staged but a previously reticent speaker like Nasser – and he was not alone among his RCC comrades – could never have play-acted such a dramatic transformation.

Perhaps power went to his head. By 1956, his closest comrades felt his distancing and several withdrew from politics. The others accepted, however much they may have begrudged it (for some, military rank was an issue), his elevated status. Nasser intuitively recognized the importance of formalizing relationships both with the people and his fellow conspirators. That meant, in addition to taking off the uniform, establishing an official decorum. For the masses, it also meant firing their spirit, and nothing was more significant than the nationalization of the

Suez Canal – a reactive but carefully considered action – and his steadfast leadership in the face of the "tripartite aggression."

The decade from 1956 to 1966 was the apogee of Nasser's influence. Time after time, seeming defeat turned into victory; even when set back on his heels he managed to remain in command. At the time, he was accused of "reckless opportunism," an "impulsive desire to be in the limelight" and of harboring a "personal desire to dominate the Arab world." Yet, in the same breath, keen observers spoke of his "courageous determination," noted that he "matured rapidly" and "established himself as an exceptionally qualified leader." [4]

In the middle of that triumphant decade, the 1961 collapse of the United Arab Republic, nine years to the day before his fatal heart attack, marked the beginning of a personal transformation. He became, according to his chroniclers, more "morose," "aloof," an "increasingly intolerant" ruler less inclined to stomach criticism, [5] no longer appreciative of political humor and "unshakably mistrustful," ever wary of conspiracies. [6] The Yemen imbroglio and the chain of mis-steps leading toward June 1967 were the culmination of a growing inwardness and inability to confront decisively those at home who, as many Egyptians passionately argued, represented the real enemies of the revolution that so many still supported. Like other political leaders who scrupulously – and sincerely – scorned personal aggrandizement and coveted power for social ends more than personal glory, Nasser proved unable and/or unwilling to confront associates, old comrades and friends who had unduly profited from their high office. In the case of Abd al-Hakim Amr, it may have been the fear of engaging in a power struggle he was not sure he could win as much as forbearance toward an ex-confidant that prevented Nasser from acting to save the military and the state.

---

[4] Wheelock, *Nasser's new Egypt*, p. 285.
[5] Stephens, *Nasser*, pp. 305–306.
[6] Lacouture, *Nasser*, pp. 361–362.

Nasser's last years were, as Muhammad Hasanayn Haykal and others have repeatedly implied, a postscript to 1967. The impact of Amr's nascent mutiny and his suicide in September 1967 undoubtedly shook Nasser, how deeply we can only imagine. Some writers, like Jean Lacouture, suggest that "as he had done so often before, when he met with a serious reverse," Nasser "tended to withdraw into a shell and, dispensing with all but the most uncritical of his associates, to take ever more responsibility upon himself." [7] Abdel Magid Farid, one of those trusted associates, admits that Nasser "was disinclined to talk and seemed deeply troubled" but counters that his "method of conducting affairs of state" changed for the better after June 1967. "He became more inclined to consult those around him, even summoning senior army officers and influential government officials who had long since retired." [8]

There was much to be done. The ceasefire between King Husayn's army and PLO militias resolved little. The Arab world, reeling from the June War, was further demoralized by the internecine horrors of "Black September." Some argued that more Palestinians had been killed by Arab forces than the Zionist enemy. Rearmament, re-evaluation of foreign policy and very hesitant steps toward reconstructing the ASU, all had to take a back seat to personal concerns for his health and thoughts for his family. Nasser spoke to confidants about retirement but he, more than they, knew that with the lack of a truly stable political order larger than his persona, this was a fantasy.

SUCCESSORS

Almost immediately on Nasser's death, the inner circle of advisers, primarily those in the ASU vanguard, handed power

---

[7] Lacouture, *Nasser*, p. 430.

[8] Farid, *Nasser*, pp. 1–2.

– as was constitutionally mandated – to Nasser's Vice President, Anwar al-Sadat. Sadat's career under Nasser had not been particularly distinguished. Never very close to the center of events, he had managed never to attract Nasser's displeasure. To his detractors, he had a reputation as a yes-man, "Major Yes-Sir" and had been a safe selection as vice president (and acting president during Nasser's absences) after the final showdown with Amr. To those who saw themselves as the movers and shakers of the future, he seemed a prudent appointment, a man associated with neither right nor left, Soviets nor Americans and outside the centers of power, the derogatory public label for those engaged in internal intelligence gathering and state security – those very people who now sought to control events from behind the scenes.

Sadat soon proved them wrong. In May 1971, having agreed to an extension of the Rogers Plan, the new President moved against his enemies. In a self-styled "corrective revolution," he had his adversaries in the ASU, military and intelligence services arrested. To great popular acclaim, he oversaw the destruction of the secret police's storehouses of wire-tapped tapes and transcripts. He promised greater political liberalization and a decisive engagement with the Israelis. In October 1973, after almost squandering his political capital by delaying a promised "year of decision," Sadat restored Egyptian honor by sending troops across the Suez Canal. With air support, and surprising the Israelis with their organization and discipline (never a feature of Amr's army) Egyptian troops took the Bar-Lev Line and chased the Israelis deep into Sinai. Concurrently, Syrian forces drove Israeli troops down the Golan Heights. Bolstered by American supplies and demonstrating superior spontaneous command, the Israelis regrouped, pushed the Egyptians back across the Suez Canal and surrounded the Egyptian Third Army on the Canal's west bank. Before this stunning turnaround, Sadat had little choice but to accept a ceasefire. Yet, from a political standpoint, Egypt's victory remained uncontested, not least by the Israelis, who embarked on a commission of inquiry that led to the fall of Golda Meir's government and a reshuffling of the military command.

"Hero of the Crossing," Sadat embarked on a major reorientation of Egypt's Nasserist economy. His October 1974 decrees ushered in the *infitah* – the "opening" of Egypt's markets to foreign investment and the dismantling of key components of the public sector. Sadat's picture now hung proudly in public squares and over shopkeepers' cash registers while Nasser's official iconic presence quickly vanished. The regime erected no statues and named no major public works project – no airport, avenue, nor government building – after him. There was a spirited public debate over Nasserism, its achievements and failings. The era had its supporters, primarily those of the left, even those who had suffered terms in prison. Yet, in a time of conspicuous consumption and the sudden availability of Western consumer goods, talk of social egalitarianism and the cries of those who could not afford the inflated prices of basic goods, largely went unheeded.

When, bowing to international pressure, Sadat cut government subsidies for basic foodstuffs, those cries could not be suppressed. The bread riots of January 1977 pushed Sadat to think more directly about hastening the disengagement of Egyptian and Israeli forces from the Sinai and ultimately led him to deliver his most stunning challenge – a willingness to travel to enemy territory if it might hasten progress toward normal relations with Israel. Two years later, after a flurry of diplomatic initiatives – Sadat's historic trip to Jerusalem in November 1977 and his September 1978 meeting with the Israeli Prime Minister Menachem Begin under American auspices at Camp David – Israel and Egypt signed a peace treaty.

Throughout the decade of "de-Nasserization," Nasser himself remained largely untouchable. The Nasserist state might be described as tyrannical – Nasser's secret police were every bit the cinematic villains that Farouk's had been – but the leader never took direct blame. The worst he was charged with, at least in official discourse (for the Muslim Brotherhood there were no holds barred) was negligence. The same was true for critics of state bureaucracy. The 1967 "setback," too bitter a pill to openly deride, had been exorcized by the October victory.

By the end of the 1970s, Sadat's fortunes had waned. His peace with Israel initially met with great enthusiasm but the lack of an economic peace dividend (Egypt, now a key part of late American Cold War regional strategy, received enhanced military aid but little that average people could touch) compounded by a resurgent, more militant Islamist movement and the perceived abandonment of the Palestinians, plunged the country into a downward spiral of political violence. Formerly a shrewd manipulator of political forces, Sadat grew careless and increasingly out of touch with political realities. In September 1981, he had over fifteen hundred opponents, of all political orientations, arrested. Within a month, on 6 October 1981, his rule had ended in a hail of bullets, at a military parade marking the eighth anniversary of the "Crossing."

His successor, Hosni Mubarak, offered renewed hope of a more democratic political order. Mubarak promised to rein in the unchecked economic liberalism which characterized Sadat's *infitah*. He brought to trial several individuals, including Sadat's brother, who had profited unduly from personal connections to the presidency. In some respects, this represented a victory for proponents of the Nasserist public sector and those who highlighted the benefits achieved by rural and urban workers under Nasser, although these hopes would later be drowned in legislation that stripped away fixed rents on agricultural land, essentially many argued, undoing land reform.

On the political front, Nasser's one-party order remained a huge stain on his reputation. By opening the political process to serious opposition parties and loosening the reins on Egypt's print media (though not broadcast media), the Mubarak regime highlighted the fraudulent nature of Nasserist and Sadatist rhetoric of democratization. As Mubarak's political reforms ossified and the country experienced an upsurge in political violence in the 1990s – primarily generated by the Islamist movement and countered by harsh state repression that did little to assuage growing public concerns about public safety and broader political outlets for the expression of popular will – the historical political failings of the Nasser era became less prominent in public debate.

Mubarak is now in his third decade of rule, his reign now longer than Nasser's. From the beginning, he has governed under emergency measures and shown little inclination to relax them or promote any clear mechanism to transfer power to a successor. In his fifth six-year term, he still rules without a vice-president. The rise to public prominence of his son, Gamal, leaves Egyptians uneasy that Egypt, like Syria (where Bashar al-Assad succeeded his father Hafiz) might find itself suddenly transformed into a dynastic republic. In early 2005, Mubarak promised to allow opposition candidates to stand for presidential elections; nine other names appeared on the ballot papers in early September. Mubarak, playing on his role as commander of the air force during the 1973 October War, campaigned under the slogan "*al-ubur ila al-mustaqbil*" (the bridge – literally crossing – to the future).

It is far too early to judge the degree to which this should be considered an historic election. The official count credited Mubarak with eighty-eight percent of the votes (amidst the usual – and not unjustified – cries of fraud and intimidation) but this should be assessed in the light of a mere twenty-three percent turnout, a new low in electoral participation. If not exactly a resounding cry of no confidence in the regime and its promises of electoral reform, these numbers suggest a disinclination to take part in political charades. As the quasi-legal Muslim Brotherhood, the largest organized opposition force in the country, was barred from fielding an official candidate (in response, the Brothers half-heartedly encouraged people to vote but endorsed no one), any attempt to gauge street sentiment will remain rooted in anecdote and intuition.

LEGACIES

When all is said and done, for those who lived under Nasser what remains is a lost sense of the heady optimism that characterized the era. Like all nostalgia propagated by a generation that sees itself as charmed – in this case the younger cohorts of the "Nasser generation" – those who came of age during it and whose world-view was shaped by the promises of his era, continue to exert considerable influence over the media, the arts and public discourse in general. Memory is selective and re-scripted to a purpose. Yusuf Chahine, Egypt's great cineaste, has long been embarrassed by his epic film, *al-Nasir Salah al-Din* (Saladin the Victorious), released in 1963. The film depicts the leader of the Muslim *jihad* against the Latin Crusaders as a pan-Arab hero (Saladin was actually a Kurd) and contains numerous textual and visual allusions to Nasser. Chahine, of course, was not alone in his enthusiasm, yet he was one of a number of high-profile directors who moved their operations to Lebanon in the wake of increasing public sector control of the film industry.

Thirty-three years later a cinematic re-enactment of Nasser's decision to nationalize the Suez Canal Company became a smash hit in Egypt, in other Arab countries (where the authorities allowed it to be screened) and amongst Arab diaspora communities in the West. *Nasser 56*, starring the late Ahmad Zaki, resurrected Nasser's populist character: a modest man of simple tastes, an incorruptible leader who ordinary citizens might approach in the streets or even telephone at home, a thoughtful man who studied a problem from every angle and worked closely with a small, capable circle of trusted advisers (not necessarily those on his ruling council) before acting. The film reintroduced many of the great anthems of the era, and touched both visual and aural chords. The state sponsored the project, yet allowed its public release in 1996 only with great reluctance for while the film reflected a supreme moment of national unity and pride, when political violence was rending the country, it also, or so Mubarak's officials feared, captured too well Nasser's charisma and reflected poorly on the current leadership. Cynics cried for a sequel that depicted Nasser in 1967, as the leader who pushed his country into the abyss of defeat. However, a series of projects treating the "setback" has been scratched for legal reasons. A later biographical film about Sadat skirted the moment (and never depicted Nasser's face, reminding some sarcastic critics of early Hollywood biblical epics).

Therein lies the complexity of Nasser's legacies. A giant of postcolonial history, a leader who embodied the popular will of his people, the Arabs and others struggling for self-determination, none the less he remained an autocrat, surrounded by corrupt and corruptible agents of state repression. An adroit manipulator of consensus, he became withdrawn, particularly in the second decade of his rule, less inclined to seek advice from experts, more comfortable with advisers of a conspiratorial mind set, even though he recognized their foibles and the danger they posed to his rule and his person.

Why did Nasser and his Free Officer comrades fail to guide Egypt toward the "sound democracy" that they promised and continually dangled before their people? The answer must combine elements of the personality, military training, political turmoil and perceived failures that dominated the officers' youths and early adulthood and, not least, their encounter with power, especially during the trying first years of rule. The officers did seize power with the intent of turning it over to, or sharing it with, civilians, especially their contemporaries, who they viewed, much like themselves, as progressive idealists. Many, especially those affiliated with embattled political parties or anti-establishment movements that sought to guide the direction of their revolution (even before they called it a revolution) disappointed them either by pushing for the too-precipitate resumption of full civilian rule or retaining loyalty to their own parties and movements. It should not be forgotten that some civilian contemporaries, as well as key legal elders, pressed the officers to further their martial ambitions. They crossed no single Rubicon but the dramatic showdowns with Muhammad Nagib and his allies, and with the Muslim Brothers in 1954, surely soured Egypt's new rulers on thoughts of opening the political process too widely too soon. The foundation and disappointing performances of the single-party mass organizations should be understood as a reaction to the officers' fears of *hizbiyya* – fractious party politics – but also in the context of contemporary popular models of political mobilization that, however flawed in retrospect, galvanized people and their leaders throughout the decolonizing world.

Throughout his political career, perhaps because of his relative youth, as well as the mythical figure he cut amongst the common people, foreign observers speculated about the extent to which Nasser might eventually settle into a more restrained, less audacious style of leadership. Keith Wheelock, writing during the heyday of the UAR, opined that Nasser, "is gaining moderation with time," having been sobered by recent "failures in Syria and Iraq" and might, "if he so chooses," "become one of the great personalities of the twentieth century, at least within the Afro-Asian world." [9] Writing shortly after his death, Malcolm Kerr emphasized the sense that Nasser's project remained unfinished and his political orientation malleable. Kerr wondered if Nasser "was preparing to render a much more genuine service to Arab brotherhood, namely a general Egyptian disengagement from Arab affairs altogether." Had he lived to do so, "he would have given proof of his greatness by renouncing one of his own principal accomplishments: the buildup in the mind of the Arab masses of the mystique of pan-Arab unity, intimately linked with their belief in the magical powers of his leadership" [10] Like so many other Western observers, however intuitive, both still viewed Nasser and Nasserism through the lenses of outsiders.

---

[9] Wheelock, *Nasser's new Egypt*, p. 285.
[10] Kerr, *Arab Cold War*, p. 156.

What did Egyptians – and Arabs – see? The photographs that once hung in government offices, schools, private shops and homes have all but vanished. They always depicted images that were more informal than regal. Usually frontal portraits, without a backdrop, Nasser smiles in almost all of them, accentuating – especially when touched-up – his amicability and common touch. In an official black-and-white portrait, probably from the late sixties, Nasser posed in profile, sphinx-like, unsmiling, with the sky behind him. This portrait highlights the grayness of his temples and the extent to which his hair color was changing. In other widely circulated pictures he walks, hand on shoulder, with his son Khalid, sits in pilgrim's garb in Mecca or shoots home movies on the beach. Sadat, in latter years, was carried away by make-believe uniforms and a self-styled pharaonic baton; after 1955, Nasser, even when he reviewed the troops, never appeared in military garb.

A man of simple tastes and large dreams. Perhaps, in retrospect, the simplicity was his prime characteristic and the dreams reflected his people's struggle for a better life. The vices, the

Legacies. A young man standing on the Aswan Dam wears a mask of the leader three decades after his death. (Photograph by the author.)

mistrust rooted in a conspiratorial background and the inflated sense of individual destiny, undoubtedly helped undermine those dreams.

To assess Nasser's place in history we must endeavor to understand the era that he dominated and the hope that he offered his people which he carried – as he was carried aloft by the masses – to the grave. In the summer of 2002, marking the fiftieth anniversary of the July Revolution, Kamal al-Tawil's and Salah Jahin's *Sura* headlined a sound-and-light show in Liberation Square. The song evoked a multiplicity of emotions amongst the producers, as well as viewers, of the gala event. To some it must have seemed a quaint historic cultural artifact, a piece of fading history, perhaps tarnished by all that came later. To some – never all – of the "Nasser generation," many of the images given life by singers and composers retain their power, tempered by historical distance but living on, despite all the subsequent setbacks. When that generation has passed, its successors must come to terms with Nasser's legacies – the great successes, the colossal failures, the still unfinished projects – and retouch the picture accordingly.

BIBLIOGRAPHIC ESSAY

Surprisingly, for a figure of Nasser's stature, there has been no authoritative biography in either Arabic or a European language in more than thirty years. The most detailed accounts of Nasser's life were written shortly after his death. The three most valuable are: Robert Stephens, *Nasser: A political biography* (Middlesex: Penguin, 1971), Jean Lacouture, *Nasser* (New York: Knopf, 1973) and Anthony Nutting, *Nasser* (London: Constable, 1972). Mohamed Heikal, *The Cairo documents* (Garden City, NY: Doubleday, 1973) contains a valuable series of sketches of Nasser on the international scene written by Nasser's adviser and confidant. Peter Woodward, *Nasser* (London: Longman, 1992), written for a "Profiles in Power" series, is the most recent short synthetic undertaking.

For a broad sweep of politics, economy, and society during Egypt's liberal era, the best, most accessible work is Jacques Berque, *Egypt: Imperialism and revolution* (New York: Praeger, 1972). Robert L. Tignor, *State, private enterprise, and economic change in Egypt: 1918–1952* (Princeton: Princeton University Press, 1984) and Joel Beinin and Zachary Lockman, *Workers on the Nile: Nationalism, Communism, Islam, and the Egyptian working class, 1882–1954* (Princeton: Princeton University Press, 1987), detail the background to the growing concerns for social equity that influenced the course of the Nasser revolution.

For the political background and early years of the Free Officers take-over, the standard work is Joel Gordon, *Nasser's blessed movement: Egypt's Free Officers and the July revolution* (New York and Oxford: Oxford University Press, 1992; Cairo: American University in Cairo Press, 1996). For the 1950s to the union with Syria, see James Jankowski, *Nasser's Egypt,*

Arab nationalism, and the United Arab Republic (Boulder, CO: Lynne Rienner, 2002). The breakdown in relations with Israel is detailed in Benny Morris, *Israel's border wars: 1949–1956* (Oxford: Clarendon, 1997). The literature on the Suez Crisis is rich; the contemporary works partisan. Mohamed H. Heikal, *Cutting the lion's tail: Suez through Egyptian eyes* (London: Andre Deutsch, 1986) and Anthony Nutting, *No end of a lesson: The story of Suez* (New York: Clarkson N. Potter, 1967), both written by people who were involved, provide good starting points; William Roger Louis and Roger Owen, *Suez 1956: The crisis and its consequences* (Oxford: Clarendon, 1989) is the most comprehensive summary to date. For Arab politics of the 1960s, Malcolm H. Kerr, *The Arab Cold War: Gamal Abd al-Nasir and his rivals* (London: Oxford University Press, 1972), is a classic. To date, the most comprehensive treatment of the June 1967 war is Michael B. Oren, *Six days in June: The 1967 Arab-Israeli war and the making of the modern Middle East* (New York: Ballantine, 2002).

Numerous academic studies have treated the political and economic contours of the Nasserist state. The most helpful are Kirk J. Beattie, *Egypt during the Nasser years: Ideology, politics, and civil society* (Boulder, CO: Westview, 1994), Charles Issawi, *Egypt in revolution: An economic analysis* (London: Oxford University Press, 1963) and Hamied Ansari, *Egypt: The stalled society* (Albany: SUNY Press, 1986). For the transformations undertaken during the early Sadat years, see John Waterbury, *Egypt: Burdens of the past / options for the future* (Bloomington: Indiana University Press, 1978).

Several important recollections by Egyptian actors in the drama are available in English: Gamal Abdel Nasser, *Egypt's liberation: The philosophy of the revolution* (Washington, DC: Public Affairs Press, 1955), Anwar Sadat, *Revolt on the Nile* (London: Alan Wingate, 1957), Mohamed Neguib, *Egypt's Destiny* (London: Victor Gollancz, 1955), Khaled Mohi El Din, *Memories of a revoltuion: Egypt 1952* (Cairo: American University in Cairo Press, 1992) and Abdel Magid Farid, *Nasser: The final years* (Reading: Ithaca, 1994). Sadat's official memoirs, *In search of identity* (New York: Harper and Row, 1977), should be noted primarily for the ways in which Nasser's successor chose to position himself as both inheritor and reformer of the Nasserist legacy.

Many foreign correspondents and academics wrote insightful accounts of the Nasser revolution as it was in progress. The best are: Jean and Simone Lacouture, *Egypt in transition* (New York: Criterion, 1958), Keith Wheelock, *Nasser's new Egypt* (New York: Frederick A. Praeger, 1960); and Tom Little, *Modern Egypt* (New York: Frederick A. Praeger, 1967).

Critiques of Nasser and Nasserism written by Egyptian opponents of the regime also abound. Anouar Abdel-Malek, *Egypt: Military society* (New York: Vintage, 1968) and Mahmoud Hussein, *Class conflict in Egypt: 1945–1970* (London: Monthly Review Press, 1973) are the most influential leftist critiques of the revolution. Ahmad Abul-Fath, *L'Affair Nasser* (Paris: Plon, 1962) is a critique of the regime's early authoritarian tendencies by a leading journalist and one-time friend. Sayyid Qutb, *Milestones* (Cedar Rapids, IA: Unity Publishing), a translation of his influential *Ma`alim fi al-tariq* (also known in English as *Signposts*) underscores the radicalization, while in Nasser's prisons, of the Muslim Brotherhood's chief ideologue. The best account of relations between the Brothers and the regime in 1954 (as well as the Brothers' origins and historical role before July 1952) is Richard P. Mitchell, *The Society of the Muslim Brothers* (London: Oxford University Press, 1969). For the aftermath, including the influence of the Nasser experience upon radical Islamism, see Gilles Kepel, *Muslim extremism in Egypt: Prophet and pharaoh* (Berkeley: University of California Press, 1986).

A recent attempt to reassess the impact and legacies of Nasserist Egpt is Elie Podeh and Onn Winckler (eds.), *Rethinking Nasserism: Revolution and historical memory in Egypt* (Gainesville: University Press of Florida, 2004). Critical cultural history of Nasserist Egypt is only beginning to be written. For the impact of Egyptian cinema, see Joel Gordon, *Revolutionary melodrama:*

Popular film and civic identity in Nasser's Egypt (Chicago: Chicago Studies on the Middle East, 2002).

The literature in Arabic, ranging from personal testimonials to narrative accounts is immense and well referenced in many recent scholarly works. The best coverage of the entire Nasser era is Ahmad Hamrush, *Qissat thawrat 23 Yulyu* (The story of the 23 July Revolution), 5 vols (Cairo: Madbuli, 1977–84). Volume 5, in particular, contains transcripts of invaluable interviews with scores of leading figures. The same is true, although in more limited context, for Abd al-Azim Ramadan, *Abd al-Nasir wa azmat Mars* (Abd al-Nasser and the March Crisis) (Cairo: Ruz al-Yusuf, 1976). The most detailed memoirs by a Free Officer founder are Abd al-Latif al-Baghdadi, *Mudhakkirat* (Memoirs), 2 vols (Cairo: Al-Maktab al-Misri al-Hadith, 1977).

Nasser's speeches and public statements have been collected in a variety of Arabic-language volumes. The major speeches are available on cassette in the Arab World, produced by Megaphone Middle East Productions (Cairo). The interview with Howard K. Smith, cited in Chapter Two, is from a duplicated cassette I either found or was given years ago. Nasser-era anthems sung by Abd al-Halim Hafiz are available on a series of cassettes released by Sout el-Phan (Cairo). I have not yet seen them transferred to CD. The complete lyrics are published by Magdi al-Imrusi, *Kurasat al-hubb wal-wataniya* (A notebook of love and patriotism) (Cairo: Sout el-Phan, 1998). The lyrics to Umm Kulthum's *al-Atlal* come from an undated collection of her songs published by Maktabat Ragab (Cairo). The feature film *Nasser 56* is available with English subtitles from Arab Film Distribution in Seattle, Washington. For the story behind, and impact of, the film, see Joel Gordon, "*Nasser 56/ Cairo 96*: Re-imaging Egypt's lost community," in either Walter Armbrust, *Mass mediations: New approaches to popular culture in the Middle East and beyond* (Berkeley: University of California Press, 2000), pp. 161–81, or Albert Hourani, Philip Khoury and Mary C. Wilson, *The history of the modern Middle East*, 2nd ed. (London: I B Taurus, 2004), pp. 579–613. The Sadat biopic,

Days of Sadat, is available with subtitles from Aramovies.com. For a comparison of the two films, see Joel Gordon, "Days of anxiety/*Days of Sadat*: Impersonating Egypt's flawed hero on the Egyptian screen," *Journal of film and video* 54 (2002), pp. 307–23.

Ultimately, this book has been shaped by many years of research in Egypt on the Nasser years and Nasser's shifting legacies. In the mid-1980s, I was fortunate to be able to discuss the origins of the Free Officers and their early years in power with many of Nasser's closest associates and most vocal opponents. In succeeding trips, I explored the cultural ramifications of the Revolution with leading figures in film, broadcast, music and publishing. Kamal al-Tawil told me the story behind the composition of *Sura*, quoted in Chapter Five, in December 1995. The many others who have helped shape my imagination of Nasser and his era have been acknowledged – never sufficiently – elsewhere.

INDEX